MANAGEMENT SKILL GUIDE

MEETINGS

Howell Parry

Croner Publications Limited
Croner House
London Road
Kingston upon Thames
Surrey KT2 6SR
Telephone: 081–547 3333

First published 1991

Published by
Croner Publications Ltd
Croner House
London Road
Kingston upon Thames
Surrey KT2 6SR
Telephone: 081–547 3333

While every care has been taken in the writing and editing of this book, readers should be aware that only Acts of Parliament and Statutory Instruments have the force of law, and that only the courts can authoritatively interpret the law.

British Library Cataloguing-in-Publication Data
Parry, Howell
Meetings. – (Croner management skill guides)
I. Title II. Series
658.4

ISBN 1–85452–071–7

Phototypeset by Intype, London
Printed by Biddles Ltd, Guildford, Surrey

Contents

Introduction

Meetings are an indispensable business tool, but they are also time consuming and, therefore, potentially time *wasting*. Avoidance of waste and improvement of productivity are as important when applied to business meetings as they are in the case of raw materials and machine running time. The aspect of cost effectiveness, therefore, looms large throughout this guide.

The word "business" is used here to denote commerce, industry, administration and services run by professional people, managers and executives, for whom meetings are part of the job. Most of the meetings which concern business people are held in-house (that is, within their own organisation or group of organisations), but a significant number are external, such as those *between* organisations and those of statutory, advisory or coordinating bodies. They all have much in common in the way they are operated, but the emphasis in this guide is particularly on domestic meetings.

Meetings enable those with common interests to have discussions, reach decisions and make announcements in a mutually convenient manner, rather than doing so piecemeal, with innumerable, overlapping transactions, a process that would be ridiculously inefficient.

It is true that some business meetings have a dubious purpose and one of the aims of the guide is to help business people to recognise and avoid them.

Time in business is precious and expensive, and meetings are notorious consumers of time. The amount of time expended on a meeting is its duration multiplied by the number of people present, plus the attendant discontinuity and the amount of time taken in planning and preparation. It is instructive to estimate the average hourly labour cost (including the non-wage element) of those attending any meeting and multiply this by their number. To be constantly aware of costs is a useful discipline in reducing the number of meetings arranged and in ensuring that they have a positive purpose and are conducted with maximum effectiveness and expedition.

Criticisms of unnecessary and badly run meetings are commonplace. But the complainants are often no better when they themselves are in charge. Meetings tend to be regarded as inevitably indisciplined and invariably time wasting. There is a feeling of helplessness which results, to a considerable extent, from failure to understand how meetings work. The purpose in this guide is to repair that gap, so that meetings satisfy three criteria for success:

(a) *purposefulness* — the aim well defined, legitimate and fulfilled
(b) *cost effectiveness* — as little waste of time as possible
(c) *participant-friendliness* — those involved find the meeting useful and satisfying.

This book is divided into ten chapters.

Chapter 1 is concerned mainly with the principles of meetings : advantages, dangers and motives, understanding of which helps those responsible to determine why and whether a meeting should be held.

Chapter 2 deals with the role of the chairman, the key factor in success or failure. Its concern is not so much with what chairmen *do* — this is covered in subsequent chapters on the more practical aspects of meetings — but with how the job should be approached: the *philosophy* of chairing, as it were.

The subject of Chapter 3 is planning, for successful meetings do not just happen: they result from knowing what has to be done to *make* them successful. The chapter explains the successive steps in planning a meeting that, properly understood, can become an automatic and, for simple meetings, virtually effortless drill.

Chapter 4 deals with the practical business of running a meeting, viewed of necessity almost wholly from the point of view of the chairman: styles of chairing and how and where they are used; pacing; control, particularly of a discussion; and, of course, closure (where weakness on the part of the chairman is a major reason for meetings going on longer than they need).

Chapter 5 takes a look at problem people, who can to a greater or lesser extent, disrupt a meeting, and how to cope with them.

In Chapter 6 the point of view of the participants is discussed: how they can help to make the meeting a success and also present their own and their department's case to the best advantage.

Efficient handling of the nuts and bolts of the meeting, the subject of Chapter 7, may not of itself ensure success, but poor administration can certainly mar and sometimes ruin a meeting that otherwise promised well.

Chapter 8 is concerned with post-meeting action, mostly preparing minutes, a matter which is often ill understood and unskilfully carried out.

Chapter 9 provides "An Instant Guide": a summary of the eight previous chapters, but sufficient in itself to be an accessible reference source.

The three appendices are based on a fictitious meeting and illustrate respectively, the agenda, anotated agenda and minutes.

The guide does not advocate slavish adherence to a laborious procedure to be used whatever the circumstances. While a set piece meeting requires for its success that certain well-established rules be followed, this is not so when, for example, an *ad hoc* group is convened to discuss a single, defined problem. But to get value for money, it is necessary for the participants, and particularly the chairman, to understand the principles on which a successful outcome is based. Those who have mastered these principles have an instinctive and unhesitating awareness of what has to be done to contribute positively and confidently to a business meeting in any capacity.

The ideas in the guide have been formed in the course of practical experience, shared with many others, of both successful and less successful meetings. Readers who believe they are already reasonably competent in the conduct of meetings may be interested to relate their own experience with the views expressed. Those who, although much concerned in meetings, do not approach them with assurance may have something useful to learn. Some may recognise themselves as transgressors in some of the ways mentioned and may be persuaded to try to reform. It is hoped that the guide will be of particular benefit to business people who are comparatively inexperienced and will welcome advice on how they can contribute to the success of any meeting in which they are, in whatever capacity, involved.

A final but important point to note is that the word "chair*man*" is used throughout. The alternatives, much used by those with sexist sensibilities, have been considered and rejected: "chairperson" on the grounds of unwieldiness and "chair" because of its comic possibilities (for example, "Where should the chair sit?"). "Chairman" and "chairmen" are well established and well understood and, in their original "old English" sense, sexless.

Chapter 1
A Meeting or Not?

The way to look at meetings is to equate them with a piece of equipment, unmatched for its purpose, but dependent on a limited and expensive power supply. The equipment is used, therefore, only when it is necessary to do so, but never to excess nor for too long at a time because there is then less power available for other purposes. It is certainly not employed for the sheer pleasure of seeing it work. And it is important always to operate it efficiently.

The power which fuels meetings is people, a scarce resource because they have other responsibilities from which meetings take them away. The more senior they are, the more onerous their responsibilities and the greater the demands on their time. Meetings at any level are not directly productive and, when they involve large numbers of staff or even comparatively few key people, the result may be complete cessation of production.

This need to balance competing demands for scarce human resources is the background against which to consider whether or not to hold a meeting. The first requirement, however, is to be clear about what is meant by a meeting.

No doubt any discussion involving two or more business colleagues is in a way a meeting, but it would be unreasonable to stretch its definition to cover every such informal gathering. The distinction is blurred, but for practical purposes a business meeting may be defined as a group of three or more people, specifically assembled for an identifiable business purpose, with the implication that success will be enhanced if appropriate disciplines are observed.

Why Meetings Are Held

Business meetings are used for a wide variety of wholly justifiable purposes, such as:

(a) to convey information or instructions
(b) to consider some subject, explore its various aspects, identify available options, and obtain opinions and reactions
(c) to determine a course of action
(d) to consult and provide an opportunity for questions
(e) to exhort, to reprimand, to warn, to encourage or to bolster flagging morale, where it is appropriate to do so collectively, rather than individually
(f) a public relations or propaganda exercise
(g) to provide an opportunity for people to let off steam
(h) formal requirements: for example, periodic board meetings
(i) semi-social occasions for purposes like presentations, announcements or conveying congratulations.

Unjustified Meetings

Some meetings have a dubious value, however. Where a meeting is purposeless, but has been called out of unquestioned habit, it cannot be justified. Where a group of executives wish to arrange a social gathering and call an unnecessary meeting so that it can be held in company time and at company expense, which is by no means unknown, their behaviour is potentially irresponsible.

Another kind of unjustified meeting is where a boss calls together a group of busy managers for a purpose which would be better served by a visit to the work place.

Borderline Meetings

The absence of a justifiable purpose is usually relatively obvious, but there are also grey areas where the participants in a meeting feel they have been assembled unnecessarily but cannot quite put their finger on what is wrong. Meetings arranged by or for people who simply like holding them are, for example, often difficult to identify: in experienced hands their purpose can be made to seem thoroughly plausible and the only real antidote is scrupulous honesty of intention by those concerned.

The problem is compounded by the fact that whether or not a meeting is regarded as justifiable can depend on the cultural environment. Thus a morale boosting meeting or one to explain some organisational change might be considered frivolous in an organisation which gave employee communications a low priority, but seen as highly important in a more enlightened organisation.

"Political" Purposes

Most elusive of all are meetings (or items on agenda) which have a "political" purpose; for example, to rubber-stamp a course of action already decided behind the scenes or, on the other hand, to rationalise postponement or evasion of a decision.

> There used to be a "joint negotiating council" in one industry whose ostensible purpose was to agree terms and conditions of employment. Up to 30 representatives of employers and unions commonly attended its meetings, a number which everybody recognised as too unwieldy for effective business. As a result, most of the time was taken up by "corridor" meetings, where a group of five or six people did the real negotiation, returning to the main meeting (whose participants had no alternative meanwhile but to wait around) for its agreements to be ratified, which they always were.

Political meetings can, of course, be completely justified and sometimes inevitable, but in a well-run business they tend to be infrequent. They should never be embarked on blindly and without recognising their true purpose.

There are three common kinds of business meeting: the series meeting, the one-off and the *ad hoc*.

Series Meetings

Series meetings involve identified groups brought together regularly for an identified purpose: committees, working parties, teams of managers or executives, consultative bodies, and so on. Meetings are the forum where their purpose is carried out. Their agenda is often lengthy and diverse and they enjoy the advantage that the participants can arrange their diaries ahead.

One-off Meetings

One-off meetings are usually convened for a single piece of business between the people concerned. It is, to be precise, more exact to describe the *group* as one-off, for there may be more than one meeting before the business is discharged. Furthermore, if these meetings continue regularly over a lengthy period, they may come to be regarded for the time being as series meetings: the dividing line is often thin. One-off meetings share with series meetings the feature that their planning can be relatively unhurried.

Ad Hoc Meetings

Ad hoc meetings, on the other hand, are by definition unpredictable and more often than not convened in a hurry. Because there is seldom time to do any detailed planning, they are liable, to a greater extent than the others, to offend the principles on which successful business meetings rely.

To understand these principles it is helpful to consider the advantages and dangers of meetings: their plus and minus points.

Plus Points

(a) Meetings enable the people concerned in a piece of business to be involved simultaneously. It is self-evident that if something affects many people it is usually more efficient to deal with it collectively than individually.

(b) Meetings enable explanations and arguments to be communicated and principles and priorities clarified to a number of people on a single occasion.

(c) Meetings enable questions to be raised and opinions, objections and emotions to be aired there and then.

(d) Well-run meetings encourage the participants to bounce ideas off each other.

(e) Meetings provide an opportunity for collective identification of views and decisions.

Minus Points

(a) Meetings can be a form of evasion: a substitute for decision or action. It is bad business practice to use a meeting as an excuse for postponing the obvious. (But this should not be confused with calling a meeting to consider once again the arguments on a difficult question that have already been rehearsed at length — do not confuse evasion with prudence.)

(b) All meetings involve an oncost of time because of factors like travel, if only along the corridor, and the time lag that occurs before any gathering gets down to productive activity. This oncost can be minimised by good organisation, but it cannot be wholly eliminated.

(c) Some of the participants (including the chairman) may without justification try to use the opportunity to clear unrelated issues.

(d) Long-windedness and other forms of self-indulgence are a continuous danger.

(e) Personality conflicts can arouse emotions and negative attitudes.

(f) Meetings intended for business can degenerate into social gatherings.

(g) Series meetings can become a habit and continue to be held long after they have outlived their usefulness.

(h) If these and other minus points are not kept in check, people with a positive outlook can become frustrated and switch off.

A Meeting or Not?

An understanding of the forms business meetings can take, their potential purposes, straight or otherwise, and their plus and minus points, is an essential basis on which to decide, when the time comes, whether a meeting is the best course of action in given circumstances. (The reference to "meetings" of course embraces individual agenda items within multi-purpose meetings.) And the final decision, no doubt after seeking appropriate advice, can come only from the person with authority in the area concerned (who is more likely than not to chair the meeting).

The best approach is to pose a series of questions, as follows.

(a) What is the purpose of the proposed meeting?
(b) Is it a legitimate purpose?
(c) Is the timing of the meeting appropriate?
(d) Is there a better means of achieving the purpose of the meeting?

These are not always easy questions and satisfactory answers call for objectivity and intellectual honesty. But they do not have to be approached laboriously: when the principles are understood, the process becomes virtually instinctive, even when time is short, as in the case of an *ad hoc* meeting.

Defining the Purpose

The basis for deciding whether the meeting should be held is to define its purpose accurately. This is also an indispensable preliminary for planning the meeting (the subject of Chapter 3); in other words, planning starts in effect as soon as the possibility of a meeting is raised.

Take the example of a proposed board meeting whose ostensible purpose was to decide whether a firm should close one of its factories. The production director approached the chief executive to arrange a date for the meeting, but the latter asked some searching questions, from which it appeared that the necessary basic information was not yet available, nor was it clear precisely what information was required. It was therefore decided that the production director should call a preliminary meeting of a few experts to examine the information question, thus enabling the main meeting to proceed, soundly based, to deal with the primary question of closure. If a full meeting had been convened prematurely, because of inaccurate definition of the immediate purpose, the lack of sufficient information would soon have become apparent, resulting in an adjournment and the need for a second full meeting.

The purposes of meetings are many and varied and they have to be defined accurately before it is possible to give a proper answer to the ultimate question whether or not to hold a meeting of the kind and at the time proposed.

The following further examples illustrate how the question should be approached.

The manager of a wages department wished to call a meeting to get colleagues' views on a change of pay day: an important matter, but, as it was not urgent, it was decided to put it on the agenda for the next monthly meeting of departmental managers.

In another organisation, departmental managers were expected to reserve Friday afternoons for a collective meeting, for which *urgent* items that cropped up during the preceding week were saved. Items for inclusion had to be notified by ten o'clock on Friday morning and the agenda distributed before lunch. No items were admitted which could be cleared by other means or wait until the following week. If nothing urgent had been notified by ten o'clock, the meeting was cancelled. Only *extremely* urgent matters were considered to justify a meeting outside this pattern.

Sometimes a meeting can create, rather than solve, problems. The interior of an office block had been rearranged and the works engineer asked the factory manager if he could call a meeting to allocate the rooms. He was told: "*You* decide the allocation and refer any complaints to me. If you call a meeting, you'll never get agreement and spend hours unproductively."

And sometimes the situation calls for more, not less. A very substantial capital investment was proposed, for which a planning department had drawn up detailed specifications and convincing reasons for spending the money. A meeting of all the interests concerned was proposed to explain what was intended. The managing director, however, took the line that several meetings spread over several weeks would be required. He explained: "It may all seem obvious and it probably is; but we have to be as certain as we can before we spend this kind of money. And, apart from that, we want everyone to be committed to this project and they won't get the hang of it first time around. You planning people have lived with this for months and know it backwards, but others, including me, need time to come to terms with it."

Deciding whether and when to hold a meeting is a matter of balancing the importance of its purpose against the time it would take. The reward for giving adequate attention to this vital primary question will be overall economy of expensive time and a solid base for *planning* the meeting.

Summary

(a) Regard meetings as a scarce resource which has to be husbanded.
(b) Meetings are not directly productive and when key people are involved production may be adversely affected.
(c) Meetings should have a positive and justifiable purpose.
(d) Between the clearly justifiable and the clearly unjustifiable is a grey area which requires close scrutiny, particularly if the purpose is "political".
(e) Meetings may be part of a series, one-off or *ad hoc*.
(f) Meetings have plus and minus points, awareness of which is important in deciding whether they should take place.
(g) The basis for deciding whether a meeting should take place is accurate definition of its purpose.
(h) Priorities and time constraints are vital determining factors in the final decision.

Chapter 2
The Chairman

In Scotland chairmen are more often than not referred to as "conveners". This is an admirable concept because it recognises the duality of their role in that they are responsible for the planning and outcome, as well as the conduct of meetings. Unless chairmen understand what they are supposed to do and are reasonably good at doing it, meetings are liable to fall short of achieving their purpose, valuable time may be wasted and participants are unlikely to feel adequately rewarded for their efforts.

Chairmen have an onerous responsibility: they are entitled to credit when things go well but must equally accept blame when things go wrong. Those who are occasionally reluctant to take the chair may not be motivated only by modesty: they may understand, at any rate subconsciously, that to do a proper job as chairman requires effort and, sometimes, a thick skin. For all that, chairing a successful meeting can be a rewarding experience.

This is not to say that others concerned in meetings have no part to play in their success or failure: they have a significant contribution to make as participants and some have important delegated functions in connection with planning and post-meeting action. But the key person at all stages is the chairman. Successful meetings do not happen of their own accord: they are *made* to happen, directly or indirectly, by the chairman.

So what is expected of chairmen?

Strictly speaking, only one of their potential functions, that of presiding over the meeting itself, is absolutely theirs alone. There is indeed the odd person, necessarily well endowed with experience and confidence, who can pick up the agenda paper, never having seen it before, and rattle through the business at a trot. It is true that these are usually formal, almost rubber stamp, occasions, where the participants want to get things over quickly.

There is one titled gentleman, with immense presence, who is the honorary president of a certain voluntary organisation. He puts in an appearance once a year at the annual general meeting and believes it his role, as do most of the participants, to complete the business in as short a time as possible. Every conceivable preparatory step is taken to facilitate his task: nominees for office, never more than one for each, have been identified; their proposers and seconders have been earmarked; and the officers are ready with their (always) brief reports. The chairman's aplomb is an entertainment in itself and his affability gives satisfaction to all.

Delegation

The above example represents a maximum degree of delegation and would be rare in a domestic business setting.

But the chairmen of many business institutions, such as advisory bodies or trade associations, also delegate to a considerable extent in that a large part of the convening, planning and follow up of meetings is in the hands of officials. The chairmen get involved as far as their time and inclination permit, but it is a reliable general rule that chairmen who know what is going on and have a contribution to make now and then are more likely to enjoy successful results than those who are wholly dependent on officials.

The chairman of a disablement advisory committee (his regular job being a steelworks executive) knew exactly where to draw the line. His contribution to the arrangements was confined to the odd original idea as to where meetings should be held and his wide local contacts opened the doors to a number of interesting changes of venue. Much of the agenda was generated by the department that sponsored the committee, but the chairman often, and with great tact, added one or two well chosen additional items. What he did insist on was to be thoroughly briefed about the conduct of the meeting, which gave him an opportunity to check, without seeming to do so, any deficiencies in the planning. Finally, he always vetted the draft minutes with great care and, when he made changes (latterly infrequently as the secretary got to know his ways), they were always apt and convincingly explained.

At the other extreme are the chairmen of small informal groups of immediate colleagues who meet to further a specific issue with little or no paperwork. These need to delegate very little in that they personally arrange the meetings, plan the order of business, decide who needs to come and prepare a post-meeting note.

The one thing that can be said of all chairmen, is that they are, by virtue of their position, in overall *control.* Naturally, sensible chairmen take advice and they often have to act within externally imposed constraints, but it is *they* who will be the main recipients of any fallout if anything goes wrong.

In-house Meetings

The principles underlying the role of the chairman are the same, whatever the nature of the meeting and whether it be internal or external. External meetings are, however, relatively infrequent and usually planned reasonably far ahead; it is domestic meetings which are the great time consumers in business life. The bulk of the meetings at which business people are liable to take the chair are domestic affairs and susceptible to domestic control, whereas the arrangement and conduct of external meetings are mostly in someone else's hands. It is, therefore, more rewarding to study the role of the chairman in a domestic context.

Apart from running the meeting, which only they can do, the chairmen of domestic meetings have discretion about which of the meeting's functions they keep in their own hands and which they delegate. The following list sets out these functions on a scale running from the maximum amount of delegation to the minimum.

At the maximum end of the delegation scale are those duties which chairmen must or ought preferably to carry out personally: they may be called direct functions. The remainder come in under the heading of indirect functions. The distinction between the two tends, of course, to become blurred around the middle of the scale.

Running the meeting	MAXIMUM
Defining the purpose of the meeting	
Deciding whether to hold the meeting	↓
Approving the draft minutes	
Agenda	extent
Deciding attenders	of
Deciding timing and venue	delegation
Monitoring post-meeting action	
Planning	↓
Administrative arrangements	
Drafting the minutes	MINIMUM

Direct Functions

The first direct duty of a chairman is to decide whether the meeting should take place and, if so, what form it should take. This has already been discussed in Chapter 1. Making a judgement on this is a matter that should rarely be delegated.

Secondly, a chairman has to take charge of the proceedings of the meeting. It is, by definition, the one function that nobody else can discharge.

The third direct job of a chairman is approval of the minutes. The point will be made in Chapter 8 that "minutes" do not necessarily have to be formal and what is needed is an adequate record which will enable all concerned to be clear about what took place. Responsibility for the form and adequacy of this record, however, rests squarely with the chairman.

Indirect Functions

Some chairmen like to do nearly everything themselves. For example, one even insisted on addressing the envelopes, his secretary having once misdirected some papers, with embarrassing results.

Overall control does not, however, mean having a finger in every pie, and getting in the way of competent assistants is one of the many unhelpful activities of which chairmen are capable.

On the other hand, chairmen are certainly well advised to appoint and, if necessary, train assistants who can be trusted to do things as they would wish, to use discretion where necessary and to refer back if in doubt. If meetings are in a regular series, such as of a committee or working party, a secretary is probably appointed to do the spadework, but it is up to the chairman to ensure the appointee is up to the job and capable of responding to guidance if inexperienced.

There are five main areas of potential delegated responsibility:

(a) determining the agenda
(b) determining timing, venue and the attenders
(c) planning
(d) the administrative arrangements and
(e) post-meeting action.

Often enough these are straightforward and obvious but, as will be seen under the heading of planning in Chapter 3, they occasionally call for delicate treatment, the need for which is not always immediately obvious. The ideal assistant is one who knows the mind of the chairman, gets on with the donkey work and can spot the potential snags which have to be referred up. The golden rule about delegation is that the chairman should not waste time on unnecessary chores, but equally not allow any dilution of *ultimate* control.

One advisory committee had a chairman, a political appointee who was not easily dislodged, who was easygoing, weak and vacillating in his approach to his duties. He, and the committee, were fortunate in having a loyal and unselfish secretary to keep the proceedings on the rails and ensure that everything went smoothly and constructively. The inevitable down side was that meetings often lasted a long time and compulsive talkers had a field day.

Who Should be the Chairman?

The inescapable consequence of the responsibility carried by chairmen is that they must have sufficient status to ensure that things can be *made* to happen. They do not necessarily have to be right at the top, although this helps and is advisable if the subject of the meeting is of real importance, but they need to have clear authority delegated from the top. It is always a mistake when a chairman is an underpowered figurehead.

When an *ad hoc* meeting is convened informally to consider some incidental piece of business, the person in charge of the matter usually takes the chair automatically. It may not be the senior person present, but it should be, at least, the senior among those who are reasonably familiar with the ground to be covered. If there is any doubt about who should take the chair, the senior person present should certainly take a hand in clarifying the position. A meeting, however informal, where nobody takes charge is half way to failure.

It is not unusual to encounter professional groups, meeting periodically to exchange experience, where the senior person declines to take the chair because of a belief in the concept of "equality" of professional status. As a result, there is no real control, peer pressure usually fails to suppress those who enjoy the sound of their own voices, discussion tends to be unstructured, and, worst of all, there is virtually no consideration of cost effectiveness.

For groups which meet at regular intervals, a designated chairman is virtually essential. The choice is more often than not obvious: for example, departmental meetings have the head of the department in the chair. But most organisations have a number of standing committees, the status of the chairman often reflecting the perceived importance of the function of the committee.

In one major company, group personnel matters used to be regulated at two levels. Policy was determined at meetings of the divisional managing directors, with the responsible board member in the chair (and the group industrial relations adviser acting as secretary). Translation of policy into action was a matter for a committee of divisional personnel managers, with the group industrial relations adviser in the chair.

Some organisations favour rotating the office of chairman for periodic meetings of colleagues from different departments or locations, as a means of training and promoting involvement. This is acceptable if the meetings are primarily intended for communication and consultation, particularly if the participants know each other well and time wasters or poseurs can be kept in order by peer pressure. There is bound to be some sacrifice of continuity and control over planning and other preliminaries, but this can be mitigated by allowing each individual to preside over three or four meetings before the next person takes over. For meetings where decisions have to be taken, however, the loss of continuity resulting from rotating the chair can lead to loss of efficiency and in these cases the practice is not advisable.

The key consideration in regard to the post of chairman must always be the maintenance of effective control over the use of an important but expensive business resource. Any other motive for deciding on a particular appointment should be subordinated to this central objective.

Summary

(a) The contribution of chairmen is crucial to the success of the meeting.

(b) The extent of their involvement depends on the degree to which they delegate. Some confine themselves to the "direct" functions connected with the meeting. Others, who delegate less, tend to get involved also in the "indirect" functions.

(c) The direct functions are broadly:
   (i) deciding whether to hold the meeting and what form it should take
   (ii) presiding over the meeting
   (iii) approving the minutes.

(d) Indirect functions, which may be delegated, with chairmen exercising ultimate control, are broadly:
   (i) determining the agenda
   (ii) determining timing, attendees and venue
   (iii) administrative arrangements
   (iv) post-meeting action.

(e) Chairmen should be of a status commensurate with their responsibilities.

Chapter 3
Planning

The key to a successful and cost effective meeting is systematic planning, the extent of which must, of course, be related to the complexity of its agenda and the time available. But the principles are identical, whether for an uncomplicated, *ad hoc* meeting, convened in a hurry, or a formally staged occasion, with ample opportunity for preparation.

The main elements of planning are concerned with:

(a) the purpose
(b) the agenda
(c) the timing
(d) the attendance
(e) rehearsal and
(f) lobbying.

For a simple meeting, these questions may have obvious answers and require little conscious thought, but they have to be considered, as in the following example.

Several vacancies occurred unexpectedly on a factory production line. The personnel manager had to take urgent measures to fill them and she decided to call a meeting to make the arrangements. Planning took only a matter of minutes, but her experience ensured that it was systematic.

The purpose was clear: to determine the steps needed to fill the vacancies.

The agenda was twofold: to deal, firstly, with recruitment and, secondly, with training.

As for *timing*, the meeting had to be held as soon as possible; she intended to ensure that the business took no more than half an hour.

She thought two people should *attend*: her personnel officer, who would be responsible for advertising the vacancies and making the initial selections, and her training manager, but the latter persuaded her that it would save duplication later if his chief instructor also attended.

Considering how to run the meeting (*rehearsal*), she recalled that her training manager tended to advocate over-elaborate training programmes; if he argued this line, the meeting would be unnecessarily prolonged.

She therefore decided to do some elementary *lobbying* and had a brief word with him to indicate that, whatever the merits of his ideas, the present situation did not allow for any training innovations, so there was no point in his suggesting them.

Planning this kind of meeting takes little time, but can save a great deal of (much more expensive) time in the course of the meeting itself. Except for the minor contribution by the training manager about who should attend, the personnel manager (the chairman) herself did all the planning, as is likely in the case of most *ad hoc* business meetings.

Where the business is substantial, perhaps multi-purpose, planning is more complex. Not that chairmen have to do it all themselves, although those who find it difficult to delegate often do more than they should, while others go to the other extreme and leave it all to subordinates.

Chairmen should be aware of what is going on and retain the last word if there are any differences of opinion, but it makes better use of resources to delegate as much as possible of the detail. Chairmen are, however, responsible for ensuring that their assistants understand and are capable of doing what is required of them.

Purpose

The overall purpose will have been taken into account in deciding whether to hold the meeting. The purpose (not only of the meeting as a whole but, of course, of individual items) remains the guiding star as planning proceeds and things can go astray unless everyone concerned is clear about it.

One well-known authority has been heard to say that the secret of an effective chairman is to steer a meeting towards an already determined outcome. Like many such cynical remarks there is a grain of truth in it.

As planning continues, the original purpose may be expanded, refined or even amended. For example, the original purpose of an item may be to reach an appropriate decision but, if it becomes apparent that the matter is unexpectedly complicated, the purpose may have to be expanded in order to ensure that the subject is properly explored. And experienced chairmen may even change course in the light of discussion, or lack of it, during the meeting itself.

Peter Drucker has related in his book, *The Effective Executive*, how Alfred P. Sloan, former Chairman and Chief Executive of General Motors, ruled at one meeting he was chairing that, since his colleagues had expressed no reservations whatever about a proposal he had made, they should postpone discussion in order to give the matter further thought. Sloan added that there were bound to be at least minor objections to his idea and he wanted to hear what they were.

The chairman of the meeting in this example expected that his proposal would be thoroughly discussed so that a decision could be taken. He postponed the item when he realised this purpose was not achievable.

Agenda

"Agenda" is a Latin word meaning "things to be done" and there is often a temptation, particularly in the case of series meetings, which may be infrequent, to try to pour a quart into a pint pot. Overcrowding is, however, unwise: to attempt too much in a given period stretches the stamina and patience of both chairman and participants and results in some items not being given the attention they deserve. Much of the agenda for a series meeting is necessarily concerned with items brought forward from a previous meeting, so a certain amount of selectivity may be necessary in accepting new items.

As in everything else, the length of the agenda has to be judged with common sense. When the participants are coming from far afield, for example, perhaps from across the world, it would be a negation of business principles not to stretch their powers of concentration a little in order not to waste their journeys.

The agenda should be notified in writing if there is time but, written or not, the prime requirement is clarity, so that the reason for the meeting and the intention behind each item is obvious to all. To achieve this, something more than a bare description of the item may be required: perhaps a reference to a previous meeting or some generally available document; perhaps a brief explanation of the business to be transacted.

It is not unknown for agenda to be left deliberately vague, with the intention of steering participants by stealth into something they might resist if they were fully in the picture. Subterfuges of this kind are unwise: they seldom work more than once or twice and are inevitably resented by the victims.

Whatever the reason, agenda for business meetings are frequently unclear and there have been instances where even the chairman has arrived with at best a vague idea of the purpose of the meeting and sometimes equipped with the wrong set of papers!

One meeting was called "to review the contract for redecorating the office". The chairman thought all decisions had been made and the purpose was to explain to those concerned what was going to happen and allow them to ask questions about the implications. Some of the participants believed, having been issued with details of tenders, that they were going to select the contractor. Others, including the person who had called the meeting (without prior discussion with the chairman), had no precise idea why they were there. In fact, the meeting was premature, as no funds had up to that time been allocated for decorating the office.

Here are some ideas about framing and ordering agenda items.

(a) There are differing views on the best place for formal or minor items, which can be disposed of quickly (sometimes called "tiddlers"). One school of thought holds that they are best dealt with at the beginning, in order to get them out of the way. Others think it is better to take the important items first, so that if time gets short it is possible to rush the tiddlers through on the nod. A somewhat cynical variation of the latter is to disguise anything controversial as a tiddler, so that it can be despatched with the minimum of discussion at the end of the meeting, when most people want to get away. These stratagems have so many pros and cons, apart from the problem of deciding what to do with borderline tiddlers, that the best way is to take agenda items in their logical order and deal with them as they come.

(b) In a series meeting the first item is usually to note the *minutes of the previous meeting*, which need be no more than a formality if they have been prepared sensibly (see Chapter 8). Items *brought forward* then follow, each carrying a reference to the previous minute number.

(c) Two useful devices are *juxtaposing* and *compositing*. The former means positioning items of a similar nature next to each other: this helps the meeting to flow in a logical sequence, as discussion of the items will often overlap. It can also make more economical use of the time of part-time attenders. Compositing consists in amalgamating one or more analogous topics into a single item. (This is a favourite means at trade union conferences of achieving a compromise between competing resolutions.)

Suppose, for example, the packaging and the labelling of a new product are to be discussed: it is clearly convenient to deal with them as a single item (compositing). If another item is concerned with changing the design of a label of a similar product, there could be advantages in the one following the other (juxtaposing).

Many experienced chairmen juxtapose or composite like items impromptu in the course of the meeting if they see advantages in doing so.

(d) It is customary and useful to invite interested parties to *submit* agenda items for series meetings. A time limit is advisable, with exemption for emergency items, as it is important to be able to filter and, if necessary, amend them before they are finally accepted. What is the point of taking pains to put the main agenda in good shape if externally sourced items are not subjected to the same discipline?

(e) Finally, the notice of agenda should be issued in good time.

An example of an agenda will be found in Appendix 1.

Supporting Information

Information related to agenda items should be relevant and adequate and it is important to ensure that the wood is not obscured by the trees. Information is not always intelligible in its raw state and may need editing in order to make it easy and quick to assimilate. It should of course be circulated to participants in good time for them to study it.

Timing

There are two aspects to this: the date and time of day of the meeting and the length of time the meeting and its individual items should take to complete (both of which are considered in Chapter 7). The passage of time is a particularly important aspect of planning. Well-judged pacing is a feature of successful meetings and this is assisted if an estimate has been made in advance of how long each part of the agenda is likely to take.

Who Should Attend?

Identifying who should attend a particular meeting is straightforward in the great majority of cases. Attendance at a meeting of a committee, for example, is self-defining, except perhaps for occasional invitees. But there are a few general rules.

(a) Keep numbers as low as is reasonable; firstly because this economises on people's time and, secondly, because the larger the meeting the more difficult it is to chair. Resist the temptation, therefore, to include specialists who have a marginal interest in a problem but "who ought to be there in case something crops up". Some senior executives also like to have assistants on hand in case they have to answer any awkward questions. This may be all very well for powerful tycoons who do not have time to master the whole of their brief, but for most people it is nothing more than expensive laziness.

(b) On the other hand, some participants may be concerned with only a limited number of items. It would be time wasting, inconsiderate and possibly inappropriate for them to be there for the whole of the proceedings. Arranging for them to attend part-time is the best solution and the order of agenda should as far as possible be planned or adjusted so that they are not kept waiting around unnecessarily.

(c) An occasional and frequently important question is who should be *excluded*. Sometimes attendance at a particular meeting can be a mark of prestige; sometimes an individual, whose attendance is no longer relevant, has continued on a committee out of habit.

It is also possible for the effectiveness of a meeting to be sabotaged by the presence of one or more subversive individuals; although their *absence* and therefore dissociation from any decision taken may, at the implementation stage, be equally damaging. Cross currents and antagonisms due to clashes of personalities are other examples of internal politics which have to be considered. There is no single answer, but there are three rules:

(i) balance the disadvantages (and cost) of *in*clusion against that of *ex*clusion;
(ii) if in the slightest doubt, consult the chairman; and
(iii) do not make too heavy weather of such a matter — there are few problems at meetings that expert chairing cannot solve.

(d) A less delicate problem is the person whose presence at a meeting would be particularly valuable but who does not wish, or genuinely cannot find time, to attend. Bring in the bigger guns of persuasion only if warranted; it is again a matter of balance.

Rehearsal

"Rehearsal" is merely a convenient word for running through the expected course of the proceedings and trying to anticipate any snags. Time may be short, especially for *ad hoc* meetings, but it is always a worthwhile exercise, even for experienced chairmen who are familiar with the subjects to be dealt with and know the participants well. Business meetings are a means of achieving business ends and rehearsing a meeting is nothing more than a method of maximising the prospects of achieving those ends. Meetings should not be allowed just to *happen*: they have, as far as possible, to be *made* to happen.

Aspects of the agenda that benefit particularly from rehearsal are:

(a) problem items and their source
(b) participants that may cause problems
(c) how problem people and items should be handled — whether any advance briefing or lobbying is called for
(d) approximately how long should be given to each item: a means of ensuring that the meeting is economically paced.

Lobbying

Lobbying consists in making preliminary approaches to selected individuals in order to identify attitudes, gain support for a particular point of view or reach an understanding about the disposal of the meeting or one of its items. Lobbying is inevitable and indispensable but can be counter-productive if handled clumsily. "Have you given any thought to X _?" is, for example, more diplomatic than "Make sure you don't support X _".

Lobbying on behalf of the "establishment" (that is, in effect, the chairman) should not be undertaken without the knowledge of the chairman. There is a real danger otherwise of lines being crossed and possibly contradictory aims being pursued. Equally, those lobbying on behalf of the chairman should carry sufficient weight to be influential.

Attempted by anyone else, lobbying may appear, possibly with justification, to be in pursuit of personal interests. On the other hand, it is perfectly normal and legitimate for participants to lobby independently as a means of furthering their *own* point of view (see Chapter 6).

Successful chairmen usually have one or more "friends" on whose support they can rely at meetings (and elsewhere). But too obvious and consistent an ally tends eventually to lose credibility. Better that discreet support is available at the right time from different individuals, as appropriate to the occasion.

It is worth noting that assistance from a "friend" can be helpful in quite minor ways, for instance, through offering a tactful interjection which enables the chairman to bring a rambling discussion to an end.

Chairmen are sometimes rightly reluctant to silence too peremptorily participants who are over-generous with their contributions.

In these circumstances, it is useful for a "friend" to suggest that the meeting "seems to be reaching a consensus" (or similar bland term), enabling the chairman to step in quickly, sum up, frame a conclusion and move on, without appearing to silence the offender directly.

Lobbying is inevitable, but, if it is haphazard, it can create more problems than it solves. The dangers are that motives may be misunderstood, intentions may be signalled, objections to a course of action may be conceived where none existed before and clear waters may be unnecessarily muddied. In short, lobbying has to be handled with delicacy and a thorough understanding of the meeting's objectives. If there is any doubt about its effects, it is best left alone.

Annotated Agenda

When chairmen are observed to be working their way with effortless mastery through complex meetings, without apparent recourse to other papers, it is virtually certain that they have arranged to be supplied with a set of notes on the agenda. These are usually called *annotated agenda* and summarise the background and purpose of each item. All chairmen value the help they get from assistants who take the trouble to learn how they like such notes to be set out. There is no standard pattern and perhaps the only general rule is to leave plenty of space so that chairmen can add any additional notes of their own. An example might be as follows.

5. *Photocopying*	Minute 28/91 refers. John Smith alleged widespread overuse. Analysis suggests not; therefore no further action.

An example of an annotated agenda will be found in Appendix 2.

Adequate planning is in the long run time saving and, while a good deal can be delegated to trusted assistants, the chairman needs to retain oversight and give personal attention to any question where there is doubt or which may significantly affect the meeting's success.

Summary

(a) The key to a successful meeting is planning, the main elements of which are the purpose, the agenda, the timing, the attenders, rehearsal and lobbying.
(b) Whether meetings are single or multi-item, the prime requirement in agenda is clarity.
(c) Agenda items are best taken in logical sequence and dealt with as they arise.
(d) Juxtaposing or compositing are useful devices where items have elements in common.
(e) Externally sourced agenda items may have to be edited before acceptance.
(f) Notice of agenda should be issued in good time.
(g) Supporting information should be comprehensible, relevant and adequate.
(h) The time element should be borne in mind in planning agenda.
(i) The number of attenders should be kept as low as is reasonable.
(j) Items which involve part-time attenders should be positioned as far as possible to suit their convenience.
(k) The presence of some individuals may prejudice the success of a meeting, but "political" considerations have to be borne in mind in deciding whether to exclude them.
(l) Rehearsal of the probable course of a meeting is a valuable means of ensuring smooth running and identifying potential snags.
(m) Lobbying can be a useful part of planning, although counter-productive if clumsily handled.
(n) Annotated agenda are a useful adjunct for chairmen.
(o) Planning should be overseen by the chairman and, while many aspects may be delegated, any question which may significantly affect the meeting's success may require personal attention.

Chapter 4
Running the Meeting

The unique feature of the chairman's job is that of presiding over the meeting. The arrangements, planning and minutes can all be done by others, without the chairman coming into the picture, however inadvisable that may be. But, by definition, only the chairman can take charge of the meeting itself.

Skilful chairing can rescue an inadequately planned meeting and unskilful exercise of this position may ruin the best planned gathering. Some chairmen are naturals, endowed with common sense, decisiveness and a flair for handling discussion, and adept at picking up the undercurrents that can sometimes divert a meeting without warning. But the skills can be acquired and the aim of this chapter is to analyse the attributes of successful chairmen and some of the problems they have to deal with.

Successful meetings have three essential characteristics:

(a) a sense of purpose
(b) cost effectiveness and
(c) participant friendliness.

Chairmen who focus on these criteria are unlikely to go far astray, whatever the pressures.

A Sense of Purpose

Successful chairmen are ever mindful of the *purpose* of the meeting and its individual items, as defined during planning (but possibly, on occasion, adjusted, if the course of the proceedings so dictates). They need, therefore, to maintain an accurate sense of direction, so that they are not unconsciously diverted from its planned purpose.

Cost-effectiveness

Judgement of pace is one of the prime attributes of an effective chairman.

An idea of the time-scale of the agenda can be worked out during planning. Within this framework the chairman has to be flexible, giving a little here and taking a little there, with an eye more on the overall trend than on each individual item.

The chairman must retain throughout an awareness that time spent at meetings is a scarce resource and that, while extension of the schedule is permissible and indeed desirable on rare occasions, time should for the most part be subjected to rigorous discipline. Business is thus kept moving, with each item and each participant getting a fair share of attention.

Good intentions do not, however, always take account of the unexpected, which may be an unforeseen item or twist in the discussion which necessitates giving the subject more time than expected. Dealing with such situations is a sure test of a chairman's effectiveness and has to take account of:

(a) the relative importance of the new element
(b) the possibility of carrying it over to a future meeting
(c) whether there is time in hand and the matter can be disposed of quickly.

Participant-friendliness

The essential constituent of any meeting is people. They are, or should be, there because they have a contribution to make to the subject, but they also have their own perceptions of priorities and outcomes, as well as their share of forebearance, vanity, loyalty, sensibility, ambition, jealousy and other human idiosyncrasies. However thorough their mastery of the agenda, chairmen who cannot get the participants at a meeting working amicably and constructively in harness are unlikely to be wholly effective. Fortunately, most participants have a positive outlook and set out, initially at any rate, to give the business reasonable attention. This is not to say that participants at meetings are uniformly cooperative. Some can be distinctly awkward and have been given a chapter of their own (see Chapter 5).

Additional Business

It is unrealistic to expect that business meetings, and this applies especially to domestic meetings, will invariably follow a perfectly symmetrical pattern. There will be occasions when it is convenient to introduce some unscheduled item, perhaps not connected with the main purpose of the meeting. *Whether* to do so is a matter of judgement and discretion on the part of chairmen (illustrating the importance of their being of a status which entitles them to make such judgements). Business moves fast, and the very fact that a certain group of executives are assembled can justify dealing with out-of-course items that have arisen unexpectedly.

> Additional items were now and then raised (with advance notification if necessary and possible) at meetings of an employment policy advisory committee made up of the divisional managing directors of a large company. The items might have nothing whatever to do with employment policy, but they were dealt with because they happened to be urgent and the assembly of these senior people was too opportune to be missed. The chairman saw to it that the practice was not abused.

While chairmen must of course keep their eye on the ball, they also have to take a "large" view. A sense of purpose, cost-effectiveness and participant-friendliness are not concepts that can be confined to a single occasion and it is ludicrous to exclude important business only because it is not on the immediate agenda.

> One particularly fastidious managing director rigorously refused to entertain unscheduled items at management meetings, but his explanation of this exclusive philosophy often took as long as it would have done to dispose of the item there and then.

A sense of proportion is also required and chairmen must insist on having the last word. They should never allow the protestations of a vociferous minority or special interest to prevail over the needs of the business, their own instincts or the wishes of the meeting as a whole. In other words, chairmen have to guard against being "hijacked".

Awareness

Chairing a meeting is hard work. Chairmen must be alert without giving an impression of intensity; dominant but not domineering. The ideal demeanour is one of effortless, but amiable, superiority. Chairmen must be manifestly in charge of the proceedings and mindful that the authority and respect which flow naturally from the position are liable to wear thin if there is any slackness in control.

> The former secretary of one important public body had the reputation of being able to run a successful meeting with the minimum of words. A colleague recalls an occasion when he had to chair a group of some 30 opinionated civil servants in overcrowded rows in a long, narrow room. His expression was warm and encouraging; his eyes ranged continuously over the group to identify those who wished to contribute; a nod of his head was usually a sufficient starting signal and a raised eyebrow an unmistakeable warning not to go on too long. His own contributions, apart from an odd, brief interim summary, were confined to names and thanks. He restricted the meeting to an hour and a half, being aware that some people had long journeys ahead. But everyone who wished to had a say, the subject under discussion was thoroughly aired and they ended with half a dozen clearly identified action points.

Although a good chairman should convey the impression of effortless mastery, attention cannot be relaxed for a moment. The one person who must remain continuously alert is the chairman.

Styles of Chairing

Meetings run in phases and successful chairmen adjust their style accordingly. Three reasonably distinct styles can be identified, often used in combination – transition from one to another being hardly perceptible in skilled hands.

The *executive* style is appropriate when it is necessary to be businesslike and decisive, to encourage progress and draw in loose ends. It is commonly used to bring the meeting to order or an item to finality.

The *relaxed* style embodies warmth and amiability; it is particularly appropriate at the beginning and end of a meeting or at intervals when it is necessary to lower the temperature or break a deadlock.

The *eductive* style is designed to draw out and encourage contributions from the participants and, since it is the style most appropriate when a subject is being explored and discussed, it is probably more extensively used than any of the others.

Take as an example a typical series meeting, which might run something like the following.

(a) The participants have arrived and are chatting to each other: the chairman asks them politely but decisively to take their places (*executive*).

(b) But the chairman then exchanges some brief pleasantries (*relaxed*) before getting down to business (*executive*).

(c) The first item is to note the minutes of the previous meeting, which is disposed of quickly, together with those items brought forward that require only a brief report back (*executive*).

(d) Two items brought forward, however, involve the presentation of information (*executive*), on the basis of which there is some discussion (*eductive*). One of the items reveals substantial common ground, which enables the chairman to sum up and confirm a decision (*executive*).

(e) The second item brought forward turns out to be more contentious and at one point the discussion (*eductive*) gets heated, causing the chairman to step in decisively (*executive*) and say a calming word (*relaxed*), before guardedly allowing the discussion to proceed (*eductive/executive*). Sensing they are not going to make progress, the chairman decides, as this is an important issue which need not be rushed, to postpone discussion until a later occasion (*executive*) – no doubt feeling there will have to be more lobbying before the matter is brought up formally again.

(f) At this point the chairman takes steps to lower the temperature and calls a short adjournment (*relaxed*).

(g) With the items brought forward disposed of, the meeting then moves on to the main agenda, the chairman still employing whatever style is appropriate to the circumstances.

(h) After completing the published agenda, the chairman invites "other business". One matter is raised which the chairman feels is not urgent and rules (*executive*), with a few reassuring words for the originator (*relaxed*), that it be included on the agenda of the next meeting. The other item calls for immediate attention, however, but the chairman ensures that discussion is brisk and leads quickly to a decision (*eductive/executive*).

(i) The chairman closes the meeting promptly (*executive*), but allows a little time for some polite interchanges with the participants (*relaxed*).

Executive Style

The epitome of the executive style might be a media stereotype of a hard headed manager: no nonsense, morally courageous, quick to size up a situation and instantly decisive. These qualities, stripped of course of any histrionics, are certainly required occasionally in an effective chairman. But used all or most of the time, an executive style would be unlikely to result in a participant-friendly meeting and might, therefore, be prejudicial to both purposefulness and cost effectiveness. It is important, more perhaps than in the case of any other, for a chairman to know exactly when and with what degree of intensity to adopt this style. There may be rare occasions, if, for example, a manager wishes to give some subordinates a ticking off, when the executive style may be appropriate undiluted, but as a general rule it is best used with as light, although still firm, a touch as possible.

There are some situations where an executive style has to be avoided at all costs, however tempted the chairman may be to call the proceedings to order.

> An ACAS conciliator recalls presiding over a meeting of trade union officials who had differing views about a particular dispute. All nine or ten present talked around the subject at length and put up all sorts of objections to the solution that was staring them in the face and at which they eventually arrived. The conciliator, his patience by this time held barely in check, asked one of the officials afterwards why it had taken so long and was told, "We had to argue ourselves into the obvious".

This was a situation where a peremptory intervention might have queered the pitch.

An executive style is particularly appropriate:

(a) to start or restart business
(b) to bring back to earth a discussion that has wandered from the point
(c) when absolute attention is required for a matter of importance
(d) when the chairman wishes, or asks one of the participants, to summarise a particular point
(e) to induce progress
(f) to bring a recalcitrant individual to order (but as delicately as possible)
(g) to close an item or the meeting itself.

The ideal executive style is crisp, decisive, clear and unemotional, the steel fist within the velvet glove being more hinted at than revealed.

Relaxed Style

This style is intended to make the participants at a meeting feel at ease, so that they behave unemotionally and constructively. It is a skilful chairman indeed who can appear relaxed while effectively exercising an executive style, and there are bound to be elements of the relaxed in the eductive style.

A relaxed style is the principle means of inducing participant-friendliness and, in helping to put the participants in a cooperative frame of mind, it contributes to both purposefulness and cost-effectiveness. But it is not synonymous with obsequiousness and does not imply any sacrifice of control.

Some of its more obvious uses are:

(a) to welcome the participants at the start of the meeting and wish them well at the end
(b) to lower any tension, not necessarily because things have got heated, but also if the participants have been concentrating intently on a complicated issue and would profit from an opportunity to slow down
(c) to deliver personal compliments or thanks
(d) at a refreshment or "comfort" break
(e) when a shy individual, perhaps a newcomer, would benefit from encouragement.

It is a mistake to think that the most successful meetings are those where noses are kept to the grindstone without relief. People *are* inclined to irrelevance, given half a chance, and they *are* prone to gossip when they get together. Some of the participants may be friends who have not seen each other for a while, so it should not be surprising if they recall old times. It would be a dull meeting without some minimum amount of "fun". On the other hand, excessive departure from strict business is obviously dangerous. Successful chairmen know precisely where to draw the line and often move deliberately into a relaxed style from time to time in order to lubricate the proceedings, so that they continue more positively when business is resumed. Some experienced chairmen have found that one of the best ways of cutting short irrelevance is to join in and then speedily return to the mainstream with an injunction on the lines of "Well, I suppose we'd better get back to business", implying that they themselves have transgressed as much as the other participants.

Eductive Style

The word "eductive" describes the act of "drawing out" and is thus particularly appropriate to phases of a meeting when the chairman wishes to elicit contributions from the participants and induce discussion. Control of discussion is the most challenging aspect of chairing because:

(a) discussion is usually the most time consuming part of a meeting

(b) it is by and large unstructured
(c) it therefore involves a higher risk of time wasting
(d) the chairman relinquishes some of the initiative to the participants
(e) diffident or uncooperative participants can slow things down.

The eductive style also calls for a degree of self-discipline on the part of the chairman, whose aim should be to stimulate rather than instigate discussion, the ideal being free flow between the participants, with only an occasional intervention from the chairman to keep the discussion on the rails and prevent it from overrunning. Yet chairmen frequently have well-informed views which appear to them, perhaps with good reason, to be more balanced than those they are hearing from participants. The temptation to intervene is often strong, but it must be resisted if the meeting is to realise its aim of being participant friendly.

One managing director had a well deserved reputation as an effective chairman and discussion at her meetings was free flowing and rewarding: but she herself said little more than a word or two of introduction of each topic.

Contrast this with another managing director whose monologues were notorious and who, having outgunned the participants at his meetings into silence, was then wont to accuse them of having no ideas of their own.

Too much talk by the chairman reduces control and inhibits contributions from the floor.

How then can chairmen best ensure that discussion flows freely and is purposeful, cost-effective and participant-friendly? They should:

(a) make it clear at the outset what the discussion is to be about
(b) sit *back* in the chair (an "overview" stance) rather than lean forward (an "intense" stance)
(c) adopt an expectant, encouraging, but unhurried, demeanour and look from one to another of the participants as though confident that they are brimming with ideas
(d) if this fails, call on an individual they know has sensible ideas but can be relied upon not to go on too long (perhaps a "friend")

(e) if necessary, pose a direct question, either at large or to an individual
(f) avoid getting into a one to one exchange with any contributor, a sore temptation if there is need to correct a misguided view (much better to wait for one of the other participants to do it)
(g) maintain continuity by "passing the cue" from one to another around the table
(h) watch for "pre-delivery" signs, which may take the form of looking intently, perhaps quizzically, at the current contributor; mumbling, as though preparing to pitch in with a remark; apparently trying to catch the chairman's eye; signalling; or a whispered remark to a neighbour
(i) allow reasonably free rein, but curtail irrelevance or long-windedness, which can often be done tactfully by means of a brief summary of the discussion so far
(j) make personal contributions as infrequent and brief as possible.

It is an education, as well as a satisfying experience, to participate in a discussion guided by an experienced hand. Furthermore, chairmen of this vintage know that, if preparation and lobbying have been done intelligently, it is usually fairly easy, without over-interference, to steer a discussion to a "sensible" conclusion.

Closure

Successful chairmen do not allow a discussion to exceed its natural span. Weak chairmen, on the other hand, are sometimes prone, having summed up and confirmed a course of action, to allow the argument to restart. But it is not businesslike to keep repeating the arguments beyond the point of decision and there is always a danger that the meeting may talk itself out of a conclusion already agreed. Like politicians, chairmen, in Dennis Healy's words, ". . . must often be content with acquiescence. . .".

It is equally dangerous and makes minute writing difficult (see Chapter 8) for business meetings to drift to an end with nobody quite sure where an item stands or who has to do what.

Effective closure of each item and of the meeting as a whole is essential and entirely in the hands of the chairman. The rules are simple and call for a clear *executive* style:

(a) step in decisively when an item has run its course
(b) succinctly summarise the main points raised and decisions reached
(c) clearly identify who is responsible for consequential action
(d) once closed, do not allow an item to be revived.

Summary

(a) Running the meeting is central to the chairman's job.
(b) The chairman should aim to ensure that the meeting is purposeful, cost-effective and participant-friendly.
(c) The executive, relaxed and eductive styles are used variously and in combination according to the phases of the meeting.
(d) *Executive*: decisive, purposeful, businesslike
Relaxed: emollient, easy
Eductive: most appropriate in leading discussion.
(e) Too much talk by the chairman reduces control.
(f) Decisive closure, with the status of each item clarified, is essential.

Chapter 5
People

People are the stuff of meetings and are a cross section of life itself: mostly amenable, if handled with reasonable sensitivity, but in a few cases liable to cause problems. As a result, without control, guidance and leadership from the chairman, a meeting may occasionally have to suffer time wasting irrelevances and diversions, and those with a positive outlook may get fed up.

Before the Meeting

Some people problems take the form of interference during planning: pressure to slant the agenda in some way advantageous to an individual; to add this or omit that.

> Head offices often have some favoured project which they would like to add to the agenda. Strong chairmen can be a great help to their planning assistants in these situations.

These activities are a corrupted form of lobbying, which it is well to distinguish from legitimate and acceptable lobbying. The answer is to have a clear conception of the *purpose* of the meeting. Woolliness about this makes it easier for the predators to insinuate themselves.

Most of the people problems, however, occur during the course of the meeting.

Trouble from the Chairman

Chairmen are the only people who can create personal problems at meetings which are virtually insoluble. The usual offenders are those who:

(a) allow the position to go to their heads and cannot resist the opportunity to show off or throw their weight about
(b) allow their personal feelings toward any of the participants to affect their conduct of the meeting
(c) treat the participants as a captive audience
(d) want to be in on everything.

Chairmen rightly hold positions of authority, which it would, except in very exceptional circumstances, be improper to challenge during the meeting. There is, therefore, little the participants can do when chairmen, through their personal behaviour, impede a meeting's success. The only solution is preventive action by someone senior to the chairman, either a word of advice or, in the absence of improvement, removal from the chair.

It is a difficult situation and perhaps the best contribution that can be made by a guide such as this is to register a warning, to which it is hoped potentially offending chairmen will pay heed.

But, to get things into perspective, it has to be said that most people problems at meetings originate with participants and about this something usually *can* be done — by the chairman.

Action by the Chairman

What do chairmen have to do to keep the participants on the rails? They start with several advantages.

(a) Most of the participants *want* to be kept on the rails: they are happier in an orderly atmosphere; they want to make a positive contribution; and they want to return to their other pressing concerns as quickly as possible.
(b) Chairmen of business meetings almost always have a firm base from which to exercise discipline because of their status and authority within the hierarchy.
(c) Most participants, even those who tend, given half a chance, to be

troublesome or uncooperative, derive pleasure from a well run meeting.

Prevention is Better Than Cure

Chairmen can help things to run smoothly and reduce the danger from problem people if they observe a few general rules:

(a) firm, polite and good humoured control from the outset of the meeting tends to discourage negative behaviour, especially if the chairman has a reputation for firmness
(b) tact and patience are the key to most difficulties
(c) neutrality is the best stance if there are internal stresses and personality conflicts
(d) the heavy hand should be used sparingly
(e) people difficulties can often be anticipated and appropriate steps taken, such as:
   (i) excluding a potential offender
   (ii) rearranging the order of the agenda
   (iii) arranging assistance from "friends"
   (iv) lobbying a potential offender, in order to convert a negative into a positive contribution.

There was to be a meeting about the draft of a revised grievance procedure and the creator of the current procedure, now in a different job, was to attend. An opinionated, eloquent, but able, character, he was likely to be critical of the new proposals, resulting in the meeting becoming at best protracted or at worst abortive. The chairman therefore appealed to the potential objector beforehand for support against "narrow minded people who might try to obstruct a fair and constructive hearing". His approach was subtle enough to gain him a supporter instead of an opponent. The chairman then got one of his "friends" to put forward at the meeting some specious arguments in favour of the old procedure, confident that they would be scornfully demolished by his new ally. His plan worked perfectly and they had a constructive discussion.

(f) a reliable way for the chairman to regain control and defuse a volatile situation is to intervene with an interim summary of the proceedings up to that point, "editing" the more extreme points of view
(g) failing this, a short adjournment may be the best way out
(h) never belittle nor deny an offender an opportunity to save face.
(i) do not judge people prematurely — a person who initially appears difficult may turn out to be perfectly sincere and constructive.

Problem People

Categorisation can be misleading, but the main types of problem people who commonly cause difficulties at meetings might be called *abstainers*, *spoilers* and *usurpers* — within each are several sub-categories.

Abstainers

Abstainers are passive spectators who not only contribute nothing but also tend to have a dampening effect on others. They can be sub-divided into the following:

(a) *The timid*
The timid require both encouragement and protection. A word before the meeting, either from the chairman or someone senior, can help. At the meeting itself timid people are more likely to respond if they receive an individual invitation to speak or answer a question, especially if it concerns a topic on which they are known to be well informed.

(b) *The aloof*
The aloof often contrive to give the impression that they are above it all; that they have better things to do than associate with lesser mortals on matters of doubtful importance.

They tend to have a hard shell and not to respond to exhortation, but chairmen must never allow themselves to be intimidated. The best solution is usually to act out an assumption that the offenders wish to be as positive as anyone else: in other words to ignore their foibles.

(c) *The inarticulate*
The inarticulate need a great deal of help from chairmen, preferably

with the cooperation of an amiably disposed fellow participant. Any help they receive has to be tactful, otherwise their diffidence can increase.

A development engineer came to a meeting to report on some research she had been doing. She knew far more about her subject than anyone else present, but when her turn came she stumbled and hesitated and made at least one factual mistake. The chairman gently asked her what advantages her discovery had over previous methods, thereby placing her on firmer ground, for she was encouraged to explain a little of what she had achieved. Then her boss, prompted by a glance from the chairman, came in with a summary ("Am I to understand you to say that . . . ?"), which led her to expand still further; and then, judging she had gained a bit of confidence, her boss posed a mild challenge to her theory, which she rebutted with some heat, disclosing a fluency which surprised even herself. An important point here is not so much that she was drawn to make a positive contribution at the current meeting, but that she received a reinforcement to her confidence for future meetings.

(d) *The uncharacteristically silent*
With participants who are uncharacteristically silent, it is not always easy to tell whether their hesitation is for personal reasons or because they are out of sympathy with the business of the meeting. It is better not to press them unduly, but a private word during a break may be helpful.

Spoilers

Unlike abstainers, who have to be drawn out, spoilers by and large have to be restrained. There is always a temptation to put them decisively in their place; but this is unwise, as it can undermine the chairmen's aim to get the participants to work as a team. Furthermore, tiresome people do not always talk nonsense and may appear tiresome because they are offering, perhaps tediously, a minority point of view, which is none the less valid and can contribute significantly to the matter in hand.

Successful chairmen learn to recognise when apparent spoilers have something useful to say and, while trying to steer them into a more acceptable manner of delivery, ensure that they are not silenced.

True spoilers fall into the following main categories.

(a) *Ego trippers*
Ego trippers can be a real nuisance, as their self-advertisement is frequently without substance. They have to be clearly but tactfully restrained (perhaps by means of a private word away from the meeting) and it is worth remembering that they are sometimes unconscious offenders with no greater fault than excessive eagerness, which it may be possible to harness positively.

(b) *Compulsive talkers*
Compulsive talkers are commonly recognised types, often treated as harmless eccentrics. Although they usually accept restraint good naturedly, it can take little to set them off again. Fortunately they tend to have sufficient sense of humour not to take offence if curbed decisively.

(c) *Filibusters*
Filibusters are fortunately a rare phenomenon. Often working as a group, they attempt to monopolise the meeting, so that constructive business is effectively "talked out". Although they are no match for decisive chairmen, filibusters can test the resolution of any who are liable to waver. They must be allowed no elbow room at all.

(d) *Snobs*
Snobs have much in common with the aloof, but prefer to demonstrate their assumed superiority overtly. Like aloof types, they have to be treated firmly but in a manner which implies that their intentions are benevolent.

(e) *Private combatants*
Private combatants who bring some personal battle into the meeting and continuously needle each other, have to be smothered at the outset. If they are momentarily discomfited, they will have little sympathy from the other participants.

(f) *Snipers*
The most dangerous breed of spoiler is the sniper, whose form of attack is destructive criticism. They are, it must be understood, rare characters, but doubly dangerous in that they are capable, if excluded from a meeting, of working subsequently to undermine decisions reached there. More often than not their guns can be

spiked by means of pressure to be specific or an incisive question. Here "friends" of the chairman can be invaluable.

Usurpers

It is always regrettable when a meeting or, more often, part of a meeting falls under the control of one of the participants, while the chairman looks on helplessly. There are two simple answers: firstly, to reduce the risk of attempted usurpation by means of firm, confident chairing; and, secondly, to nip any actual attempt swiftly in the bud. The former holds good whatever the circumstances, but the latter is sometimes easier said than done.

It is not too difficult to deal tactfully with one who is more or less on an equal footing with the chairman and juniors should cause no problems, but the offenders are too often seniors who join the meeting as "observers" and then seek to make use of it for purposes which sometimes have nothing to do with the intended agenda.

Only the most self-disciplined senior can resist the temptation to intervene in a meeting run by a junior, especially where the chairman's control is uncertain. There is, however, no point in trying to compete with a senior who has the floor. All a chairman can do when a usurper is a senior is to step in decisively and regain control at the first opportunity. Most senior people are capable of getting the message if they have overstepped the mark and see that the chairman has a clear idea how the meeting should be conducted.

The golden rule is never to allow more than one meeting at a time.

Inattention

Inattention does not really come within the "problem" category. It is neither a serious offence nor one exclusively committed by difficult people. It is not to be expected that all the participants at a business meeting will give all the items all their attention all the time. Minor instances of inattention (or *apparent* inattention — a person may be listening intently while appearing to be immersed in some documents) are bound to occur regularly, without any action being taken or called for by the chairman. On the other hand, general inattention needs to be corrected, but at most nothing more is likely to be needed than a quiet word or gesture.

A Sense of Proportion

The importance or influence of those who can to a greater or lesser extent disrupt a meeting must not be exaggerated. Happily, extreme examples occur infrequently, but people with a *tendency* to be abstainers, spoilers or usurpers turn up fairly regularly. A successful chairman needs to be able to recognise them and know what to do, and indeed *whether* to do anything, to control them. It usually requires no more than a modest signal but most of the other participants will observe what has happened and take heed.

Summary

(a) Some people problems occur during the planning phase of meetings.
(b) Chairmen themselves sometimes cause personal problems at meetings.
(c) Most participants at meetings behave positively, but a minority can cause trouble.
(d) Chairmen have advantages arising from status and the fact that most participants are on their side.
(e) Problem people are best controlled by a mixture of firmness, tact, good humour, patience and neutrality.
(f) If problem people are identified beforehand it may be possible to take steps to reduce their impact.
(g) Difficult situations can usually be defused by means of an interim summary or an adjournment.
(h) Problem people include abstainers (those who hold back); spoilers (those who disrupt); and usurpers. Excessive inattention also needs to be corrected.
(i) A chairman has to judge whether the nature or seriousness of any problem makes remedial action necessary or practicable.
(j) Participants are far less likely to try anything on with a chairman who has a reputation for exercising firm control.

Chapter 6
The Participants

While the linchpin of a meeting is its chairman, its participants also have a substantial part to play in its success. It has already been noted that obstruction on their part can hinder the efforts of a good chairman and their support rescue a weak one. Equally significant, however, is the quality of their contribution to the business of the meeting: what they can offer by way of information on a proposal and opinion on its implications; whether their views are soundly based or superficial; whether their ideas are well or ill-expressed. Their contribution has to be judged also from the viewpoint of how adequately it helps their department's and their own aims.

It follows that planning is by no means the prerogative of the chairman and staff. It is not enough that the participants should turn up promptly, behave themselves and speak up as helpfully as possible when the occasion arises. Purposeful, cost-effective and participant-friendly, in short, successful, meetings are more likely to be achieved by team effort, with the chairman at the helm backed by a good crew. The participants, therefore, have to do their homework.

Departmental and Personal Aims

Business meetings often expose, and are intended to expose, conflicts of interest between departments and individuals, according to their function. For example, in considering a new process, the views of a safety manager may be at odds with those of a production manager; a company accountant's approach to an advertising budget may well be more prudent than a marketing manager's; or a branch manager may have more ambitious ideas about staffing levels than an area manager. The decisions reached at meetings will be sounder if departmental and individual attitudes to each item have been pithily expressed and constructively reconciled. This does not mean of course that everyone present is expected to have something to say about every item, but it does mean that in preparing for a meeting, the participants have to clarify the reason for their presence and their line on those items that concern them.

In some cases, an individual's role at a particular meeting may be immediately obvious. But in other cases detailed consultation with departmental head or colleagues may be called for. Here are some of the things that have to be taken into account.

(a) The first requirement is to be clear about the purpose of the meeting (and its individual items). The agenda may not always make this plain; if not, participants must try to find out; and in doing so they may well make their first contribution to the success of the meeting, for their enquiries may help to clarify other minds.
(b) The next step is to consider to what extent the agenda items are of personal and departmental concern. Is there a departmental view or interest and, if not, are they matters on which there *should* be a departmental line? On the other hand, are any of the items of merely peripheral or no interest?
(c) What are the strengths and weaknesses of any departmental views?
(d) What line are other departments likely to take about these items?
(e) Are there any additional items that might be contributed to the agenda?
(f) Is there any supporting material that could assist the proceedings? If so, is this readily available or does it need to be specially prepared — and would the time cost of preparation be justified by its usefulness?

Aspects of Planning

Planning for a meeting by the participants is not necessarily a lengthy process. How much time is spent on it depends on the degree of departmental and individual interest and commitment. It may also depend on how well a participant's department is organised and its policies defined. Furthermore, little or no preparation may be required by participants whose interest is marginal.

The following may be useful as a check list.

(a) Any contribution to the agenda or supporting material should be submitted in good time.
(b) Consider whether it would be helpful to do any lobbying.
(c) Ascertain or, if this is not practicable, try to anticipate, the viewpoint of other participants on particular aspects.
(d) If two or more departmental representatives attend a meeting, ensure that they have a common position, so that they are not in the predicament of having to reconcile internal disagreements as they go along.
(e) Consider whether possible contributions to discussion should be drafted in advance? Would notes be useful? Would any research be appropriate? If the contribution is complex, is it important enough to justify preparing an *aide memoire* (the shorter the better) for the benefit of others?

A production manager was invited to attend a meeting whose subject was "Stress". She remembered reading an article on stress prevention, which she thought would be worth mentioning, but unfortunately failed to refresh her memory about the precise measures the article recommended. When she duly mentioned the article at the meeting, there was some interest and she was invited to enlarge on her remarks, but she dried up and her opportunity passed.

(f) Those who wish to be sure they get a hearing should have a prior word with the chairman.
(g) Participants should read their papers as thoroughly as possible before the meeting.

Conduct at the Meeting

Here are some simple suggestions which may help participants to contribute more effectively to the success of the meetings they attend.

(a) Participants who wish to speak should not hang back. If they wait too long their opportunity may have passed.

(b) Aim for clarity and brevity, qualities which come more easily if contributions have been prepared beforehand.
(c) Be constructive; do not show off; help the chairman; do not get drawn into side meetings; and do not be put off by spoilers.
(d) Those who are not sure at the end how an item stands should get it clarified.

The Company Perspective

The need for participants to understand their role and to plan intelligently is even more pertinent at meetings between separate organisations than at domestic meetings. Inadequate preparation, to say nothing of individual blunders and unreconciled differences of view, may do no great harm if kept within the family; but in a more public arena any such shortcomings can seriously damage company interests.

In his book, *The Second World War*, John Keegan points out that at the Casablanca Conference American acceptance of the British point of view ". . . was due almost exclusively to . . . [the fact that] . . . the British party had come prepared. They had . . . agreed a common position in anticipation of events; unlike the Americans, they did not have to thrash out their internal disagreements as they went along".

Participant Responsibility

Too many business people go to meetings, complaining beforehand of the time they take and afterwards of their ineffectiveness, having themselves done little to make a constructive contribution. The complainants are likely to be as guilty as anyone else of all the faults — inadequate control, time wasting, interruptions, long-windedness, disorder — they profess to find so irritating. They should remember that it is not the responsibility of the chairman alone to ensure a successful meeting.

Summary

(a) Participants should make sure they understand the purpose of the meeting.
(b) They should clarify their own and their department's attitude and, if appropriate, the attitude of others to the meeting's business.
(c) Any agenda items and supporting material should be submitted in good time.
(d) Advance preparation of proposed contributions and advance study of documents are always worthwhile.
(e) Participants who wish to speak should go in determinedly, but should be sparing and brief with their contributions.
(f) Behave courteously and constructively.
(g) At the end, get clarification of any item where the outcome is not plain.
(h) Understanding of their role and effective planning by participants is even more important in meetings involving other organisations than in internal meetings.

Chapter 7
Nuts and Bolts

Murphy's law proclaims that if anything *can* go wrong it *will* go wrong. So it is with meetings and particularly the *arrangements* for meetings – the nuts and bolts. Something goes wrong sooner or later for even the most efficient organiser, resulting in varying degrees of inconvenience, annoyance, additional cost, loss of concentration and probable, if concealed, participant *un*friendliness.

Human failings are one thing, but some administrative shortcomings, during both preparation and proceedings, which often spoil an otherwise satisfactory meeting, are due to lack of foresight or planning. There is immense value, therefore, in developing a well understood routine, so that when a meeting is contemplated, the nuts and bolts fall automatically into place, with clear definition of who does what.

Where and When

It would be an unusually self-effacing chairman whose personal convenience did not play some part in determining where and when a meeting should be held. But self-interest aside, in business the chairman's time is likely to be more in demand and therefore more expensive than anyone else's, so it is not unreasonble, other things being equal, to expect the participants to put their own preferences in second place. On the other hand, it is hardly businesslike and certainly not conducive to a successful meeting for a chairman to take no account at all of, or worse, ride roughshod over, the convenience of others.

The core determinants are the location and availability of the key participants and the urgency and importance of the purpose of the meeting. Some or all of the following questions have to be taken into account.

(a) If the participants are coming from several places, where are most of them located and how far do they have to travel? Making economical arrangements amounts to a minor logistical exercise. It may, for example, be more convenient and less time consuming in some cases to hire a midway meeting place.
(b) What is the best date for most people?
(c) What other commitments do the chairman and key participants have?
(d) To what extent can the meeting be timed or located to fit in with their other engagements?
(e) If they are heavily committed, can the business wait or is it of low enough priority to allow the meeting to be cancelled or postponed indefinitely?
(f) The date and location of series meetings should be arranged at the latest during the previous meeting. It is even better to fix them for several months ahead. Many organisations find it convenient to have a predetermined pattern for all their series meetings, thus ensuring there are no overlapping dates.

Many business people, often highly paid and important, spend a great deal of time travelling unnecessarily long distances to attend comparatively low priority meetings. Generous dividends can accrue, therefore, if a reasonable amount of care is taken deciding whether, when, and where a meeting should be held and who should attend.

Notification

The rules about notification are so simple and the benefits of compliance so obvious that it is remarkable they are so often neglected.

(a) Send notifications, with agenda and other documents, in as good time as possible. A brief advance note about time and place is particularly useful to participants who have other commitments to consider. Try to give an hour or two's warning even of urgent *ad hoc* meetings.
(b) Cancellations and postponements, although occasionally unavoid-

able, are disruptive and the nearer the meeting, the greater the disruption. The convenience of chairman and senior participants alone is seldom adequate justification.

(c) Tell the participants how long the meeting is expected to last.

(d) Tell part-time attenders approximately what time their item is expected to be reached.

(e) Recheck that agenda and supporting material are clear and complete.

Accommodation

The meeting room should be as comfortable, commodious and quiet as possible, not too small and also not too large for the number expected. Seating should not of course be positively *un*comfortable, but people *are* liable to nod off if their chairs are too well upholstered. Ensure that heating and ventilation are as good as can be managed.

The shape of the table can be important: square is better than long and thin, and round is best of all; try to give people plenty of space for their bits and pieces. It is well worth taking the trouble to rearrange the furniture if it is clearly inconveniently placed.

A meeting was being arranged in an hotel between the management of a large engineering company and its trade union representatives, with an ACAS official in the chair. 20 or more people were involved and the hotel was asked to provide a "good sized room", with a round or square table, for a "sizeable number". On arrival they found they had been accommodated in the ballroom, with a table in a hollow square big enough for 50 people. The chairman took matters into his own hands and persuaded the party to turn themselves into furniture removers and in ten minutes a more compact setting was provided, although nothing could be done about the wide open spaces of the ballroom. As it happened, the joint removal exercise broke the ice very effectively and they were able to get down to constructive business rapidly.

Meetings held in someone's office, even if suitably furnished, are, if possible, better avoided. Interruptions and other diversions are less likely away from the immediate work environment. When offices *are* used it is worth giving attention to the arrangement of the furniture.

Where the number of participants is too large for a table to be accommodated, it is best to arrange the seating in as near a horseshoe shape as possible. It may have to be a shallow horseshoe, but the more the participants can see of each other, the better it is for the give and take of discussion, and the easier the job of the chairman.

Sometimes, of course, the number may be so large that there is no alternative but seating in rows. This may be all very well if the main purpose of the meeting is communication (for example, a manager briefing the workforce). But if the purpose is to induce discussion, the question must arise whether a series of smaller groups, more suitably disposed, would be preferable.

Prearranged Seating

It is always worth considering whether seating should be prearranged, in order that, for example:

(a) those likely to play a prominent part in the meeting have a prominent place
(b) potential problem people can be kept under the chairman's eye, or
(c) well known conspirators or adversaries can be kept apart.

Name cards are necessary only for larger, formal meetings; otherwise an invitation by the chairman to take such and such a seat is sufficient.

In business situations, ideal accommodation is all too often not available, but it should always be a rule to take a little trouble to arrange the best possible facilities.

Equipment

Equipment, such as visual aids, is often needed at business meetings, especially if there is to be a presentation. Apart from such special provisions, however, it is always convenient to have a flip chart or similar display equipment available, for illustrative use or to make notes of the stages of an argument, which all can see.

Interruptions

Take steps, as far as possible, to reroute telephone calls and prevent interruptions.

Refreshments

Reasonable provision of tea, coffee and food, if the meeting is prolonged, can give the participants renewed sharpness if they are getting jaded. If not already arranged, it may be helpful to call for refreshments when it appears that a break would be welcome. Apart from the opportunity to relax, this can sometimes be a useful tactical move. It is preferable, if possible, not to continue business while people are taking refreshments, especially a main meal.

Smaller Meetings

Many business meetings do not of course call for much formal organisation, but the principles still hold good.

Punctuality

Wise chairmen insist on punctuality. There is no greater time waster than people arriving in dribs and drabs and this is what inevitably happens when chairmen take no notice of latecomers or, worse, are themselves late. Chairmen who have acquired a reputation for strictness in this respect rarely have problems. Make it a rule that anyone who is unavoidably held up should send a message. Do not keep part-time attenders waiting too long, even if it means adjusting the agenda.

Natural Breaks

Ensure that there are "comfort breaks" at reasonable intervals, a practice which can avoid much discomfort and loss of concentration. Otherwise people will sooner or later be compelled to excuse themselves, one usually following the other until there is a spontaneous break in the proceedings.

Chairmen sometimes forget that, when they are concentrating on the meeting, as they should be, their own natural processes are liable to go into temporary suspense, in contrast to those of the less committed participants.

Smoking

The question of smoking is one where many organisations have firm policies. If not, it is a matter chairmen should face and decide one way or the other.

Duration

As a general rule long meetings are self-defeating: the participants get bored, lose their concentration and wholly or partly switch off. They are also liable to suffer from diminishing cost-effectiveness. It is bad enough when the reason is an excessive amount of business, but worse when meetings are prolonged because there is too much repetitive talk, as a result of poor chairing.

Lengthy meetings are justified only where busy and important people have travelled significant distances from widely separated locations and where, because of the high cost of actually getting to the meeting, it would be wasteful not to get through as much business as possible and continue longer than would normally be acceptable.

Minutes

Preparation of minutes is dealt with in Chapter 8, but it has to be decided beforehand *who* will be doing the minutes. It is sufficient to say at this stage that it is *not* a chore for an inexperienced junior. Minute writing requires adequate background knowledge of the business of the meeting and, in the case of series meetings, whoever does it should be given the opportunity of gaining proficiency over a reasonable period. The practice, which is common enough, of passing responsibility for minutes to whichever reluctant participant can be dragooned into the task is a bad one. Standing committees should have an appointed secretary of appropriate status. But it is otherwise up to the chairman to ensure that minutes are done by a capable person who is likely to make a successful job of them.

Summary

(a) There is need for a well understood routine for handling the nuts and bolts of meetings.
(b) Where and when a meeting is held depends on its urgency and importance and the location and availability of the key figures.
(c) Notifications and other documents should be clearly drafted and despatched in good time.
(d) Accommodation should be the best available.
(e) Housekeeping arrangements should be made in good time.
(f) During the meeting adequate attention should be given to punctuality, avoiding overrunning, comfort breaks, refreshments and the rules about smoking.
(g) Overlong meetings are usually self-defeating.

Summary

Chapter 8
After the Meeting

The Need for a Record

Meetings are a means to an end and much of the time and effort expended in convening, planning and holding them is wasted if afterwards the chairman, participants and others concerned do not have the means of confirming what happened, in respect of:

(a) factual details
(b) the main arguments advanced
(c) decisions reached
(d) postponement, if any, and its reason
(e) consequential action
(f) responsibility for consequential action.

However expertly the chairman has ordered the proceedings and however well prepared and attentive the participants have been, memory is never wholly reliable. Are there any business people who cannot recall occasions where some action arising from a meeting was overlooked? "I didn't realise I was supposed to do it," is a familiar cry.

The absence of an adequate record of meetings is frequently the cause of time wasting, mistakes, duplication, inaction and evasion of responsibility. If a meeting is worthy of being held, it is worthy of a record. Simple and brief *ad hoc* meetings might conceivably be an exception, but only then if there is no possibility of misunderstanding or implication for the future.

Meetings cannot be regarded as successful unless there are means of effective follow-up, which is not possible without adequate records.

Minutes — or a Note

Records of meetings are usually called minutes. The word itself may be off-putting: perhaps it has an institutional flavour, implying an obligation to follow a prescribed formal pattern. "Writing the minutes" is perceived as an inherently formidable task and a challenge to be avoided, if possible.

For many meetings, nothing more is required than a simple note. Minutes, in the generally accepted sense, are unnecessary for the majority of *ad hoc* or one-off meetings, especially when they are single item.

Take as an example a short meeting to decide how and when to announce a management reorganisation. The note might run:

> Note of meeting 29.6.90 (John Smith, Mary Webb, Tom Tucker, Jack Horner) re management reorganisation announcement — postpone until after holidays; Friday best, therefore *7.9.90*; warn no gossiping meanwhile; action JH.

Half a dozen words may suffice, but one thing that must never be omitted is the *date*.

> An employer and a trade union were at odds about a certain work practice. It was common ground that
>
> (a) this had originally been a temporary variation from normal working and
>
> (b) work practices that had continued for over three years became a term of contract.
>
> The employer contended that more than three years had elapsed; the union said less. The simple solution was to check the note of the meeting where the temporary variation was agreed: it was found that the note was quite explicit but *undated*.

The point at which notes become minutes is unimportant: both serve the same purpose and are governed by the same principles. The best way of covering most of the eventualities, therefore, is to discuss the preparation of records on the basis of formal minutes as applied to series meetings with multi-item agenda.

Preparing Minutes

It has already been suggested (see Chapter 7) that minutes are not a chore for an inexperienced junior, as their preparation calls for a thorough knowledge of the substance of the meeting and its participants. For series meetings, continuity is also important and the practice of taking turns to do the minutes hardly ever works. The best person to do the minutes of one-off and *ad hoc* meetings is often one of the chairman's immediate assistants and, where only a brief note is required, it may well be the chairman personally who does it. It is certainly the chairman who has to make clear whose job it is.

Groundwork

A large part of the groundwork for the minutes is done during the planning phase and it is a good general rule that the more thorough the planning, the easier it is to write the minutes. Much time can be saved after the meeting and the minutes done much more quickly if the minute writer has already assembled an outline covering items such as:

(a) a provisional list of attenders
(b) the overall form of the minutes, probably based quite often on a standard pattern
(c) any formalities (eg congratulations to an attender on some note-worthy event)
(d) clearance of any report-back item which is likely to be dealt with summarily.

Any text prepared in advance must of course be changed if things do not turn out as expected, but amendments are likely to be relatively minor.

Action at the Meeting

Minutes have, of course, to be based on notes taken during the course of the meeting. Some inexperienced minute writers may have doubts about their ability to keep up with the proceedings; they may worry that they will miss something. They will find in practice that, provided *they are familiar with the subjects of the meeting and know something about the participants*, they will cope perfectly well. It is more important for a minute writer to understand what is going on than to have a note of every last word of the proceedings. Insurance in the form of a shorthand writer is seldom necessary.

The minute writer's first draft of the minutes should not in any case be the last word, as it should be vetted by the chairman and at least some of the participants before it is adopted as the definitive text. Effective chairmen make their own notes of the more significant points and have the final responsibility for accuracy. (See the section on "Closure" in Chapter 4.) A case could be argued for the *chairman* being the minute writer: who else, it might be said, is in a better position to prepare a valid record? This is reasonable enough for an uncomplicated single subject meeting, where only a straightforward note is required; but for anything more, the chairman has to give full attention to the priority task of controlling the proceedings.

The secretary of a standing advisory committee presided for over a year between chairman appointments and decided to continue as minute writer during this period. The arrangement worked well enough, mainly because he and his colleagues were experts in their subject and had collaborated closely for a long time; business was despatched expeditiously and all played their part constructively. But he believes in retrospect that it would have been better all round if a temporary secretary had been brought in.

The Form of the Minutes

The overall aim of minutes is to record *as briefly as possible* the conclusion reached in each item of the meeting and, as far as necessary, the discussion that led to the conclusion. Organisational conventions may vary, but effective minutes are likely to conform to the following rules:

(a) Apart from the date, the minutes should be headed to indicate briefly *what the meeting was about*. Thus not "Minutes of Meeting Held 1 April 1991" but "Launch of Product X – Minutes of Meeting Held 1 April 1991".

(b) List the attenders in alphabetical order (which disposes of any argument about precedence).

(c) Minutes relating to items brought forward should have a reference to the previous minute number and, unless it is clear from the context, give a brief indication — as a memory jogger — of the substance of the matter. For example, the sense of "*Canteen* — It was decided not to go ahead with this proposal," is not immediately obvious. A more comprehensible version is: "*Canteen* — It was decided not to go ahead with the proposal to install a new pressure cooker."

(d) The conclusion and any consequential action should be stated explicitly and unambiguously. For example: not "It was decided to accept the recommendation and take action accordingly" but "It was decided to build an extension to the main office, within a budget of £1 million, as set out in Plan X (see Appendix B), and that a sub-committee, comprising Mary Martin, Peter Potts and Sally Smith, should prepare specifications, invite tenders and select a contractor."

(e) The person or persons responsible for any action should be named.

(f) The discussion which led up to the conclusion should be summarised to the extent necessary for future reference. This is important in the case of both positive and negative conclusions, in order to avoid the possibility of doubt or duplication in the future. A convenient way of summarising a discussion is to list the main arguments. Personal references are necessary only to identify a crucial contribution to the question or where one individual view carries particular weight. For example:

The main points of the discussion arising from Mary Martin's report were
A
B
C (suggested by Chief Executive)
D.

(g) As a general rule, any significant minority view should be recorded. This does not mean that a note need be made of every minor objection to a course of action, only those which, if generally accepted, might have resulted in a different decision.

(h) It is important that minutes should be easy to assimilate and understand. Brevity, clarity, avoidance of irrelevance and repetition, pruning of unnecessary adjectives and adverbs and the use of commonly understood language all assist this. It is also advantageous if minute writers have a good prose style, so that their texts are pleasant to read. Great literary efforts are not, however, called for.

(i) Verbatim records may sometimes be appropriate where statements have to be recorded precisely (and, if so, a shorthand note is essential, preferably reinforced with a tape recording), but for the generality of business meetings they are quite unnecessary and result in minutes being unduly lengthy and opaque. Equally superfluous are records of the pleasantries which are properly used to lubricate the proceedings, although it is permissible to include any personal references of particular significance. For example: "The chairman congratulated John Jones on his election as captain of the works cricket team."

But to mention virtually every passing comment is uncalled for and can be taken to the point of caricature.

The minutes several years ago of a national wage negotiating body began as follows: "The Chairman, beginning on a light note, observed that the newspapers that day had reported inflation in Germany as being negative and in competition with such a situation perhaps the employers' offer at their earlier meeting had been too high! (Laughter). Mr . . . retorted that for all the offer was worth it might as well have been withdrawn; it had cost more to circulate to his members than its value. (More laughter.)" The final sentence of these minutes included the following: "In concluding the formal business of the day, the Chairman . . . invited the trade union side to join the employers for lunch." Asked why the minutes were in this form, the secretary at the time agreed they included a lot of padding, but said "we have always done them this way".

Old fashioned styles of minute writing such as the above have continued out of habit in some organisations. The only way to get rid of them is by decisive executive action. Any initial dismay will quickly be replaced by a pleasurable relief.

(j) Appendices are usually the most convenient way of recording complex material, such as a report or opinion delivered orally at the meeting, which is pertinent to the conclusion of an item, but too lengthy to be set out in detail in the body of the minutes.

(k) Minutes should be set out in a manner and sequence which allows easy comprehension. Thus the business of the meeting does not necessarily have to be recorded chronologically; it might, for example be logical to amalgamate two or more separate items which turned out to have elements in common. Likewise, items which were separate on the agenda, but were for convenience taken together, might equally be covered by a single minute.

(l) Agenda items which are found to have no substance need be recorded only if the lack of substance is itself significant. A hardy annual in most agenda is an item designated "Any other business" and some minutes include a wholly superfluous reference on the lines of "*Any other business* – There was no other business".

(m) Minutes should be numbered. A convenient method for series meetings is to start numbering at the beginning of each calendar year and continue the sequence throughout that year – thus the first meeting of the year might start with "Minute 1/91" and end with "Minute 23/91"; and the second meeting then start with "Minute 24/91"; and so on. This enables a minute to be traced quickly and avoid the alternative of referring, for example, to "Minute 20 of the meeting held on 11.4.91".

An example of a set of minutes will be found in Appendix 3.

Urgency

The underlying theme throughout this guide is that meetings should, because of their cost, be treated as a scarce business resource, to be used only to further matters of importance. It follows that the record of a meeting should be available to those concerned as soon after the event as possible. There are, unfortunately, many instances in business where preparation of minutes is delayed too long, often for no other reason than a distaste for paperwork. Not least of the chairman's many responsibilities is to ensure that minutes are given first priority by the minute writer and a close timetable, strictly followed, can be a useful means of ensuring this.

Cabinet minute writers work in relays, so that the minutes of the early business are already being written up while the rest of the meeting continues. Another example of proper urgency is one well known company where the company secretary starts on the minutes immediately after board meetings, working into the early hours if necessary to ensure that the first draft is in the chairman's hands first thing in the morning.

Finalising the Minutes

It is vital that minutes should be an accurate reflection of what happened at the meeting and it is both unfair and unwise to leave their final form in the hands of the minute writer. The person with final responsibility is the chairman, to whom the first draft should go for approval and, if thought necessary, amendment.

Inexperienced minute writers sometimes get annoyed if their efforts are, as they see it, "hacked about" by chairmen, still more if the amendment relates to style rather than accuracy. They forget that they probably have much to learn from practised hands and also that chairmen are likely to have good reasons, perhaps of a "political" nature, unperceived by others, for preferring one form of words to another. In the course of time (another benefit of continuity) minute writers get to know how chairmen like the minutes written and find the amendments get fewer and fewer; those who fail to get the message are unlikely to do the job successfully.

In some business circumstances, for example where the chairman is the appointee of a senior executive, the latter may wish to have the final say about the minutes. Assuming, however, that the chairman has the last word, is this as far as it should go? Should other key participants also have a sight of the draft minutes before they are finalised? The answer must surely be that, if the possibility of an occasional, perhaps harmful, mistake is to be avoided, it is essential for key participants to be consulted, at any rate about those items that concern them. In the case of a one-off meeting, of course, the "minutes" or "note" may be drafted and the approval of the participants obtained there and then.

All these stages in the process of finalising the minutes must, it goes without saying, be completed with urgency.

In the company referred to above, where the company secretary has the first draft ready early the next morning, the chairman does his part within an hour or two and the draft is faxed to the other directors later that day, with a very short deadline for any objections, so that the final version of the minutes is despatched little more than 24 hours after the meeting. Any snag over a particular detail that takes longer to clear is not allowed to hold up the rest: the minutes go out with a note that the final version of "Minute _ will follow as soon as possible".

Distribution

It should go without saying that, once finalised, minutes should be distributed speedily, but to whom? To the participants of course, but there may be others interested in the business of the meeting who would find it convenient to have copies. On the other hand, minutes of high level meetings often contain confidential material, knowledge of which should be confined to a select few. The solution is to provide copies of the full minutes only to those entitled to be privy to the whole of the business transacted at the meeting and give relevant extracts to those with a part interest or responsibility for action.

Action on Minutes

Minutes should be noted so as to make it clear who has to do what, with a deadline date for completion of the action (eg "action Tom Piper by 30.6.91"). It is also good practice for the minute writer, or other executive designated by the chairman, to monitor the progress of the required action and, if the meeting is one of a series, ensure that a report back is on the agenda for the next meeting.

Action on the minutes deserves the same sense of priorities as other aspects of the meeting. It is not, however, unknown for certain individuals, including at times chairmen themselves, to delay, and even keep in indefinite suspense, action on decisions about which they have reservations.

In one organisation, the management committee decided to introduce a management appraisal system, against the advice, for whatever reason, of the personnel director, who then became responsible for implementing the decision. Determined not to give in

> without a struggle, however, he went through the necessary motions at a progressively slower pace. Since there was no effective monitoring system and the other directors had their own preoccupations, the management appraisal programme was allowed to fall into limbo and disappeared from sight until uncovered many years later by a new and more positively motivated personnel director.

Meetings will sometimes fail to achieve their intended purpose and individuals may attempt to manipulate them in various ways for their own and even for what they see as legitimate corporate ends. These dangers can be significantly minimised if meetings have adequate records, which are precisely and promptly prepared, distributed and followed up.

Summary

(a) There should be a dated record of what happens at meetings, except for *ad hoc* assemblies of transitory significance, in order to avoid misunderstanding, for use as an action memo and for future reference.
(b) A brief note may suffice for uncomplicated single item meetings.
(c) Minute writing calls for experience, knowledge of the subject and participants, and, for series meetings, continuity.
(d) Preparatory work on the minutes can save time later.
(e) Minutes should be numbered and record, in precise, readable language:
  (i) the conclusion reached for each item
  (ii) who is responsible for any action and
  (iii) a summary of the discussion which led to the conclusion.
  References to personal contributions are usually unnecessary, except for significant minority views.
(f) Verbatim records are appropriate only in special cases and extraneous happenings of no significance should be excluded.
(g) Accounts of supporting material considered at meetings should, if a record is necessary, be relegated to appendices.
(h) Analogous items may be amalgamated under one minute heading.
(i) Minutes should be prepared and distributed promptly.
(j) Post-meeting action should be positive, prompt and monitored.

Chapter 9
An Instant Guide

The central aim of this guide has been to provide a reasonably comprehensive analysis of the main components of a successful business meeting, which it is hoped will be useful not only to beginners but also to those whose experience is substantial, but who would welcome a yardstick against which to compare their own ideas.

Some business people, however, may wish merely to sharpen their skills or have an easily accessible reference source.

There is probably a place, therefore, for an "instant" guide, which summarises the salient features of a meeting in sufficient, but not excessive, detail. The present chapter sets out to provide such a guide. Those who have absorbed the contents of the previous eight chapters may safely skip this one, unless they make use of it as an overall summary or a quick means of revision.

There are seven sections:

1. Basic Principles
2. Planning
3. Running the Meeting
4. Problem People
5. The Participants
6. Nuts and Bolts
7. Post-meeting Action

Section 1 – Basic Principles

Before going into the mechanics of organising and running a meeting, four basic considerations have to be addressed:

(a) the characteristics of meetings
(b) the decision whether or not to hold a meeting
(c) the determinants of a successful meeting
(d) the role of the chairman.

The Characteristics of Meetings

Meetings have the following characteristics.

(a) Properly used, they are an indispensable business resource.
(b) Some are unnecessary and their value may even be negative.
(c) They are an expensive and time-consuming resource.
(d) They are not necessarily the best way of dealing with a particular issue.
(e) They have advantages and disadvantages, for example:

(i) advantages
- they enable business to be dealt with collectively
- they provide an opportunity to raise questions and differences
- they allow mutual exchange of ideas between the participants;

(ii) disadvantages
- they can provide a plausible excuse for evading action
- they can be an occasion for self-indulgence or abuse by the participants
- they can become a habit.

A Meeting or Not?

With these characteristics in mind, someone – usually the *chairman*, perhaps acting under orders from above and frequently seeking advice from colleagues – has to decide whether or not to go ahead with a prospective meeting.

The following questions have to be answered objectively and each item in the proposed agenda should be subjected to similar scrutiny.

(a) What is the purpose of the meeting?
(b) Is it a justifiable purpose?
(c) Is the timing appropriate? (A meeting may, for example, be called prematurely, before information essential to its business is available.)
(d) Is there a better means of achieving the purpose of the meeting?

Once the principles are understood, these questions arise automatically, even when time is short.

The Determinants of Success

Successful business meetings are those which are:

(a) *purposeful* – in that the meeting has a well defined purpose and a clear and constructive outcome
(b) *cost-effective* – in that the organisation's time has been well spent
(c) *participant-friendly* – in that the participants feel satisfied with the proceedings and the way the meeting's conclusions were reached.

The Chairman

Chairmen are the linchpin of meetings, be they informal *ad hoc* gatherings or formal set-piece affairs. They are the determining factor in the conception, conduct and outcome of meetings.

A meeting without a designated chairman is unlikely to be successful, because it is liable to be convened uncritically, to proceed with no sense of direction and to lack a clear end-product.

The degree of the chairman's involvement may range from merely presiding over the proceedings to doing virtually everything. As a general rule, however, the chairman should, while exercising overall control and accepting final responsibility, delegate as much as possible to responsible assistants (without getting under their feet).

A chairman should be of a status commensurate with the responsibilities and, if not the boss, at least the direct appointee, vested with the authority and backing, of the boss.

Section 2 — Planning

The success of a meeting results to a large extent from the quality of the planning, the basic principles of which do not vary, however straightforward or complex the business in hand. For a simple *ad hoc* meeting planning may amount to no more than a few minutes' thought by the chairman, but for a more formal set-piece occasion, much of the detailed planning is likely to be delegated, with the chairman available to resolve any doubts. Bodies which hold a succession of meetings usually have a designated secretary. Chairmen should ensure that controversial planning decisions are referred to them.

The main stages of planning are concerned with the agenda, timing, the attenders, rehearsal, and lobbying. At each stage the *purpose* of the meeting (and each of its items) should be borne firmly in mind, although the original purpose may sometimes be modified as planning proceeds.

The Agenda

(a) The prime requirement is clarity, with the aim of ensuring that the participants are not taken by surprise and are able to come as fully prepared as possible.
(b) For a simple meeting, a few lines may suffice and, if time is short, the agenda need not be in writing.
(c) The items for multi-agenda meetings (see the example in Appendix 1) are best taken in logical sequence, but it is sometimes useful to amalgamate items that have elements in common.
(d) Supporting information should be comprehensible, relevant and adequate.
(e) Notice of the meeting should be issued in good time.

Timing

Planning the timing is important because it is part of the chairman's job in running the meeting to ensure that it is evenly paced, with adequate attention given to important items and the minimum of time taken by lesser items. Estimating timing is an invaluable part of planning and contributes significantly to a smooth running meeting.

Attendance

Determining who should attend a meeting is a matter of holding a balance between:

(a) keeping the numbers as low as possible (in the interest of cost-effectiveness) and
(b) ensuring that those who have a real contribution to make are not excluded.

Some of the attenders may have to be present only for those items that concern them. For these, as well as other part-time attenders (for example, specialist advisers), an attempt should be made to adjust the order of the agenda, so that they do not have to wait around unnecessarily.

Rehearsal

Rehearsal means nothing more than the chairman, with, if necessary, the planners and key participants, running through the business of the meeting in order to identify possible snags and consider how to handle the main items. For important meetings it may be a substantial exercise, but for routine occasions it need take little time.

To go into a meeting without such rehearsal, however, can result in unforeseen snags and will, in addition, almost certainly cause the meeting to continue longer than necessary.

Lobbying

Lobbying consists in having preliminary consultations with people likely to influence the course of the meeting. It usually amounts to no more than an exchange of views or a request to one of the participants to take the lead in some aspect of discussion. It may, however, create misunderstandings if it is haphazard and may rebound if clumsily handled.

From the chairman's point of view, it can be a useful means of identifying "friends", who can be of help in keeping the meeting on the rails if there are any difficulties.

Annotated Agenda

This final aspect of planning can be helpful to chairmen in running a meeting of any complexity. A handy note on the agenda items, any incidental business and significant personalities, is much easier for the chairman to cope with than a voluminous dossier on each item. (See an example in Appendix 2.)

Section 3 — Running the Meeting

Running the meeting is the one job that is exclusive to chairmen and they can never afford to lose sight of the three yardsticks which determine success:

(a) purposefulness
(b) cost-effectiveness and
(c) participant-friendliness.

With these principles in mind, their best course is to:

(a) stick to the agenda
(b) pace the meeting so that each item or aspect gets a fair share of time
(c) be flexible in dealing with unexpected developments or additional business (it may, for example, save time in the long run to deal with an unscheduled — or even unrelated — item there and then, rather than carry it forward)
(d) be attentive and alert, intent on ensuring that the participants work together as a team, while remaining the undisputed arbiter of events
(e) be sparing with their own contributions.

Styles of Chairing

Meetings run in phases and successful chairmen change their styles according to the needs of the occasion. For example, they may:

(a) adopt a businesslike and decisive style if they wish to keep the meeting to the point
(b) take a more relaxed line if they wish to set the participants at ease or to lower the temperature
(c) adopt a manner which will draw out the participants if they are leading a discussion.

Experienced chairmen fall into these changes of style subconsciously, the transition being hardly perceptible in skilled hands.

Discussion

Discussion imposes the biggest challenge in chairing a meeting, because it:

(a) is relatively time consuming
(b) tends to be unstructured
(c) involves relinquishing some of the initiative to the participants
(d) requires chairmen to exercise self-discipline, their aim being to encourage free flow *between* the participants.

In guiding a discussion, chairmen should:

(a) clarify its purpose and bring it back on the rails if it has wandered from the point
(b) watch for individuals who appear to have something to say
(c) if there is initial silence, call on an individual known to have ideas on the subject
(d) alternatively, pose relevant questions, either at large or to an individual
(e) avoid personal exchanges with individuals, aiming instead to pass opinions around the table
(f) tactfully curtail long-winded contributions
(g) make personal contributions brief and infrequent, ideally confined to interim summaries, if the discussion is prolonged, and a final summing up.

Relaxation

Most chairmen find that to allow an occasional brief light-hearted irrelevance or item of gossip enables the participants to relax and is beneficial to the progress of the meeting.

Closure

Decisive closure of the meeting (and of each item), with a clear summing up of the conclusions reached and definition of responsibility for further action, is essential.

Section 4 – Problem People

The impact of problem people must not be exaggerated, as most of them merely have a *tendency* to the shortcomings described and are usually responsive to a quiet signal from the chairman, but a small minority can occasionally cause problems at meetings.

Chairmen should always remember that:

(a) they have the authority to lay down the law if necessary
(b) most participants have a positive attitude and are potential allies against the more troublesome
(c) it helps to make it clear from the outset who is in charge (while remaining polite, good humoured, tactful, and patient)
(d) preventive steps – such as rearranging the agenda or lobbying – may be wise if an item is potentially difficult
(e) they are in a position, if matters look like getting out of hand, to intervene with a (tactfully worded) summary of progress or, as a last resort, to call a short adjournment.

The main categories of problem people and what can be done about them are as follows.

Abstainers

There are people who hold back and include:

(a) the *timid* and the *inarticulate*, who have to be encouraged
(b) the *aloof*, who can be intimidating, but whose foibles are best ignored
(c) the *uncharacteristically silent*, who may have a personal reason for their reticence and should not be pressed unduly.

Spoilers

There are people who have to be restrained and include:

(a) *ego-trippers*, whose offence is often nothing more than excessive eagerness, which can usually be harnessed positively
(b) *compulsive talkers*, who usually accept restraint good humouredly
(c) *snobs*, who try to demonstrate superiority and whose attitude is, like that of the aloof, best ignored
(d) *filibusters*, who try to spoil the meeting by monopolising it, and *snipers*, whose speciality is destructive criticism, both fortunately rare, but needing to be put down firmly
(e) *private combatants*, whose mutual antagonism has to be neutralised from the outset.

Usurpers

Usurpers are those who try to take over or start a separate meeting. If they are juniors or peers, they need not pose a problem. The real trouble comes from seniors, who sometimes like to "sit in" at meetings and are liable to intervene with irrelevancies. They usually have to be tolerated and the only real solution is to step in decisively and regain control at the first opportunity. There are two golden rules:

(a) minimise usurpation by conducting the meeting decisively
(b) do not allow more than one meeting at a time.

Inattention

Inattention is not strictly a "problem", except when it is general, which may indicate boredom or tiredness, conditions certainly requiring action by the chairman.

Section 5 — The Participants

Participants have a significant part to play in the success of the meeting and may find the following guidelines helpful.

(a) They should plan for the meeting by ensuring they are fully aware of its purpose.
(b) They should clarify and test the strengths and weaknesses of their department and their own views on its items.
(c) If two or more departmental representatives are to attend, they should ensure that they present a common viewpoint.
(d) It may be helpful to sound out the attitude of other interested parties and tactful lobbying may be appropriate.
(e) A succinct background paper may be a useful reinforcement of a particularly important point of view.
(f) Any contributions to the agenda should be submitted in good time.
(g) At the meeting itself, they should behave constructively and ensure that their contributions are clear and as brief as possible (perhaps prepared in advance).
(h) They should ensure they are clear about the outcome of each item.
(i) These considerations apply particularly in the case of meetings involving other organisations.

Section 6 — Nuts and Bolts

A well understood routine, with responsibility clearly defined, can minimise administrative failures, which often spoil an otherwise satisfactory meeting. Here are some guidelines.

(a) The decision where and when to hold the meeting should take account of overall convenience, particularly that of the chairman and key participants.

(b) Notification and related paperwork should be distributed to those concerned in good time.
(c) Accommodation should be as comfortable, commodious and quiet as possible.
(d) Steps should be taken to minimise interruptions.
(e) Adequate attention should be given to refreshments and personal needs.
(f) Punctuality is important; part-time attenders should not be kept waiting too long; the proceedings should be kept as short as possible.
(g) The minute taker, if any, should be a competent person, adequately briefed.

Section 7 — Post-meeting Action

Post-meeting action should be prompt and positive; otherwise the purpose of the meeting is liable to be frustrated. The two main aspects are preparing a record of the meeting and taking action on decisions reached; here are some guidelines.

(a) All but the simplest, *ad hoc* meetings need a *dated* record, written by someone familiar with the subject-matter of the meeting, as a reminder to the participants and for future reference.
(b) A brief note often suffices, but proper minutes are required if the proceedings are complex.
(c) Minutes and other records should make clear the conclusion reached, responsibility for action, and, unless the reasoning is clear, a summary (hardly ever a verbatim account) of the discussion on which the conclusion is based. If they relate to a multi-item meeting, they should be numbered and set out in a manner and sequence which allows easy comprehension.
(d) There should be no avoidable delay in preparing, checking and distributing minutes.
(e) Action arising from the meeting should be carried out as quickly as possible by the persons designated. Machinery for monitoring may be desirable in complex organisations.

Chapter 10
Conclusion

A Scarce Resource

The starting point of this guide is the proposition that business meetings are a scarce, expensive and time consuming, although essential, resource: scarce because their participants have many other urgent preoccupations; expensive because of the aggregate salary costs and discontinuity involved; and time consuming because meetings are a human activity, which cannot be mechanically programmed. Yet this resource is regularly treated as though it were plentiful, cheap and provided with an inexhaustible supply of time.

A Successful Meeting

The guide goes on to introduce the concept of a successful meeting, defined as one that is purposeful, cost-effective and participant-friendly. Success in this context, it is suggested, is based on understanding the nature of meetings, particularly the role of the chairman, and on planning and running meetings in a systematic and controlled manner.

The Demands of Modern Business

These concepts may be attractive and convincing in theory; the question has to be faced, however, whether they are practical propositions in the real world of business. Put it another way: is the culture of relatively unorganised meetings, which exists in many organisations, too ingrained to make a more rational pattern a feasible objective? Rather than make a systematic attempt to improve the conduct of meetings, it might be said, would it not be more realistic to accept that meetings are by their nature imperfect and the most that can be done is to approach them with a bit of common sense and control them as well as possible in the circumstances of each?

The objection to such a *laissez faire* approach is that the business world is speeding up, demands on the time of managers and executives become greater every day, while the penalty of mistaken decisions can be disastrous. There can be little or no slack in modern business and meetings that are not "successful" run the risk, like other examples of inefficiency, of turning out to be expensive liabilities.

More Meetings, Not Less

Because of the complexity and technological sophistication of business organisations and the pace of market competition nowadays, decision making calls for greater agility and coordination than formerly. Vastly more computer generated information is available, which has to be interpreted and evaluated. An additional number of meetings at management and executive level seems likely to be an inevitable consequence.

There is the further factor that those employed in business have developed greater individual self-reliance and more independent motivation and are less prepared to accept orders from superiors or so-called professional experts on trust. They expect to be informed and consulted, and experience tends to indicate that well informed employees, at all levels, are better motivated and give a better return for their pay than those who are content to do unthinkingly as they are told.

It seems then that meetings of all kinds are going to become more, not less, prolific, which makes it even more important that they should earn their keep.

Available Models

It so happens that many employee meetings provide a useful model of the way meetings ought to be approached. Because of their nature, they tend to be reasonably well controlled and seldom take an excessive length of time, although it would be self-defeating if they were too obviously rushed. Their aim, after all, is to communicate a sense of purpose to junior employees, which would hardly be achieved if the meetings were taken at a gallop. On the other hand, an idle or unsupervised production line or office is a powerful incentive to keep them as short as possible.

Another good model is available in the out of hours meetings many business executives attend in connection with various voluntary activities, for example, their professional associations. Those who attend such meetings must be struck by the way they quickly get down to business and how there is no unnecessary waste of time: time that the participants no doubt feel could be better spent on leisure pursuits or with their families.

Business meetings involving two or more organisations also tend to be comparatively well conducted, perhaps because they have been better planned, usually have the benefit of a more experienced chairman, and perhaps also because the participants are on their best behaviour in the company of strangers or rivals.

Domestic Meetings

The area which would benefit most from improvement is that of domestic meetings involving middle and senior people. To narrow the focus still further: *ad hoc* and one-off meetings are probably bigger offenders than series meetings, for which there is likely to be at least a rudimentary planning structure.

This should not be taken to imply that most domestic *ad hoc* and one-off meetings are at the lower end of the quality scale and most external meetings tend towards the upper end, with domestic series meetings somewhere in the middle. Generalisations are always dangerous and experience suggests that a significant number of *all* categories of business meetings are capable of improvement. Domestic meetings, especially of the *ad hoc* and one-off variety, are, however, the category in which business managers and executives are most involved. These are the great time consumers, which are most likely to disrupt their working lives and retard their effectiveness.

The Target for Improvement

It is reasonable, therefore, to identify the main target for improvement as in-house meetings arranged at comparatively short notice between middle and senior grade business managers and executives. This is also likely to be a particularly rewarding and influential target because the effectiveness of this group of people in regard to almost any business skill is central to organisational success. Get these meetings right and there is a good chance that the others will fall into place.

Resistance Factors

The reasons why participants in the target group may be resistant to therapy probably include the following.

(a) However intent they may be on running a tight meeting if left to themselves, they are reluctant to appear over-punctilious among their peers.
(b) Many of them do not organise their schedules particularly effectively, with the result that time for forward planning is at a premium and they regard preparation for meetings as expendable. (Although it does not affect the "bottom line" as obviously as cash liquidity, "time liquidity" may be an almost equally significant factor in business efficiency.)
(c) Attending meetings, grumble as they may, is seen by many as a welcome escape from the hectic daily pace; an hour of relaxation with congenial colleagues away from the demands of customers and subordinates.
(d) They have a sense of inevitability about the futility of meetings.

But, sweep all these impediments away, if it were possible, and there remains the decisive probability that many business managers and executives genuinely do not understand, firstly, how meetings tick and, secondly, what they have to do to improve their effectiveness. This guide offers them a means of repairing these omissions.

Motivation to Improve

But managers' first task is to convince themselves that improvement *is* both possible and desirable. Their most likely motivator is money. One revealing discipline is to log the aggregate gross time taken in attending meetings over a reasonable period and set it against the estimated average salary costs (including non-wage elements) of those concerned. It will be a source of comfort if the result appears reasonable and it may then be a useful form of management development to identify the reason for such a comparatively happy state of affairs.

If, on the other hand, the result of the investigation gives cause for concern, the incentive to take therapeutic measures will be compelling. The most useful approach is to break down the figures in respect of those who have chaired meetings during the period of the investigation and compare the records of each. Identifying the critical group of offenders is always a more accurate remedy for an organisational ill than taking global action which embraces the comparatively innocent as well as the guilty.

One way or the other, successful meetings are a goal worth striving for and the path to the goal is worth mapping. The aim of this guide is to provide the means of preparing such a map.

Appendix 1

(The model agenda, annotated agenda and minutes in Appendices 1, 2 and 3, respectively, relate to the same fictitious meeting.)

MURDSTONE AND GRINBY plc

Group Headquarters
1 March 1991

To: Rosa Dartle – Frozen Foods Division
Jack Maldon – Wines and Spirits Division
Clarissa Spenlow – Group HQ
Henry Spiker – Catering Division
James Steerforth – Cereal Products Division
Thomas Traddles – Retail Outlets Division
Mick Walker – Transport and Warehousing Division

PERSONNEL COORDINATING COMMITTEE

It is confirmed that the next meeting will be held at . . . . . . on 1 April 1991, starting at 10am. The agenda is set out below.

Agnes Wickfield
Secretary

AGENDA

1 MINUTES of the meeting held on 10 January 1991
— Already distributed

Brought Forward Items

2 CENTRALISED TRAINING (minute 68/90 refers)
— To consider report of sub-committee, already distributed

3a. EMPLOYEE HANDBOOKS (minute 10/91 refers)
— Progress report on preparation of guidelines

3b. EMPLOYEE MEETINGS (minute 11/91 refers)
— Proposal to extend quarterly shop floor meetings (as already introduced in Catering Division) throughout Group

(The two above items to be taken together, because of overlapping interest.)

4. PAY NEGOTIATIONS (minute 13/91 refers)
— Progress report

5. NEW STYLE PAY SLIPS (minute 17/91 refers)
— Progress report

New Items

6. RECRUITMENT AGE LIMITS
— To discuss Chief Executive's wish to review recruitment of job applicants over 50 (copy CE memo enclosed)

7. VIDEO LIBRARY
— To discuss offer by XYZ Training Videos of free showing of two 15 minute training videos ("Stress" and "Alcoholism")

8. CRAFT APPRENTICE AND GRADUATE TRAINEE INTAKE
— To discuss instruction by Chief Executive that rate of craft apprentice and graduate trainee intake should be maintained

9. COMPUTERISATION OF TRAINING RECORDS
   – Talk by Ms Anne Markleham, ABC Consultants, on recent developments

   (Item 9 to be taken at 12.30, Ms Markleham remaining for lunch.)

10. EMPLOYEE DISCOUNTS
    – To discuss discrepancies between divisions in rate of employee discounts (item submitted by JS)

11. OTHER BUSINESS

12. NEXT MEETING
    – Provisionally arranged 10am, 4.7.91 at . . . . . .

MURDSTONE AND GRINBY plc

Group Headquarters
27 March 1991

To: Rosa Dartle – Frozen Foods Division
Jack Maldon – Wines and Spirits Division
Clarissa Spenlow – Group HQ
Henry Spiker – Catering Division
James Steerforth – Cereal Products Division
Thomas Traddles – Retail Outlets Division
Mick Walker – Transport and Warehousing Division

PERSONNEL COORDINATING COMMITTEE MEETING – 1.4.91

I enclose a copy of a letter Catering Division has received from LMN Finance. The Chairman proposes that we should have at least a preliminary discussion of the matter, depending on time.

Agnes Wickfield
Secretary

Appendix 2

PERSONNEL COORDINATING COMMITTEE MEETING – 1.4.91

ANNOTATED AGENDA

Jack Maldon, new PM, W&S Division, attending for first time.
Ms Anne Markleham, ABC Consultants, to give talk on COMPUTERISATION OF TRAINING RECORDS: invited for 12.30 (adjust agenda as necessary) – remain for lunch.
Apology: TT (unwell – too late to arrange deputy)

1. MINUTES 10.1.91	Distributed

Brought Forward Items

2. CENTRALISED TRAINING (estimate 10.05)	Minute 68/90 (11.10.90 meeting) Sub-committee (HS/MW/AW) Report (distributed) recommends centralisation not feasible because of diverse divisional circumstances
(Take 3a and 3b as single item)	
3a. EMPLOYEE HANDBOOKS (estimate 10.30)	Minute 10/91 Preparation of guidelines under way

	— draft to divisions about 6 weeks
3b.EMPLOYEE MEETINGS	Minute 11/91 You favour quarterly shop floor meetings (on Catering Division pattern) throughout Group. Need for caution — many line managers lukewarm (? training) — differing divisional circumstances (eg T&W). Perhaps start with experiments.
4. PAY NEGOTIATIONS (estimate 11.00)	Minute 13/91 All completed — confidential summary distributed.
5. NEW STYLE PAY SLIPS (estimate 11.20)	Minute 17/91 No problems reported. Little discussion expected. ? short break.

New Items

6. RECRUITMENT AGE LIMITS (estimate 11.30)	CE's memo of 25.2.91 (copies distributed) asked you to consider whether traditional attitudes are detrimental to applicants over 50. ? small working group to investigate.
7. VIDEO LIBRARY (estimate 12.00)	XYZ Training Videos have offered free showing of two 15 minute training videos ("Stress" and "Alcoholism"). Could be useful in Video Library.
8. APPRENTICE/GRADUATE INTAKE (estimate 12.05)	PMs will support CE view that apprentice/graduate intake should be maintained, despite cutbacks. Main problem to overcome resist-

ance in divisions, intent on immediate budgets.

9. COMPUTERISATION OF TRAINING RECORDS (timed for 12.30)

Talk — Ms Anne Markleham, partner ABC Consultants.
Formerly wide training experience in . . . . . . Commission.
ABC programmes said to hold records and plan individual training "path". Some of our existing records may need tidying up before computer will accept.
ABC fees for feasibility study apparently reasonable, but software expensive.
(Ms Markleham remaining for lunch.)

10. EMPLOYEE DISCOUNTS (estimate 2.00)

JS has suggested uniform rate throughout group.
FF and CP divisions enjoy higher rate of . . %.

11. OTHER BUSINESS (estimate 2.20)

One late item notified (participants informed) — FINANCIAL ADVICE TO EMPLOYEES. Catering Division has received offer from LMN Finance to provide advice at nominal charge to employees coming into money (eg RP). HS suggests uniform Group line. Danger biased advice.
(Pursue item depending on time — some wish to leave 3.00 latest.)

12. NEXT MEETING

Provisionally arranged 10am 4.7.91 at . . . . . .
You have another meeting — switch to *5.7.91* if OK for others.

Appendix 3

MURDSTONE AND GRINBY plc
PERSONNEL COORDINATING COMMITTEE
MINUTES OF MEETING HELD ON 1 APRIL 1991

PRESENT Clarissa Spenlow – Group HQ (Chairman)
Rosa Dartle – Frozen Foods Division
Jack Maldon – Wines and Spirits Division
Henry Spiker – Catering Division
James Steerforth – Cereal Product Division
Mick Walker – Transport and Warehousing Division
Agnes Wickfield – Group HQ (Secretary)

APOLOGIES Thomas Traddles – Retail Outlets Division

The Chairman welcomed JM to the Committee and congratulated him on his appointment as Personnel Manager of the Wines and Spirits Division.

23/91 MINUTES
The minutes of the meeting held on 10 January 1991 were noted.

Brought forward items

24/91 CENTRALISED TRAINING (minute 68/90 refers)
It was decided, as a result of the report of the sub committee (HS, MW & AW), not to proceed with the suggestion that all employee training should be centralised under Group auspices. (Summary report: Appendix 1)

25/91 EMPLOYEE COMMUNICATION (minutes 10/91 and 11/91 refer)
Preparation of guidelines on divisional employee handbooks (10/91) has started and a draft is to be sent to divisions for comment in about six weeks. [Action: AW by 11.5.91]

It was the general view that quarterly shop floor meetings, on the lines of those already introduced in Catering Division (11/91), would be beneficial throughout the Group, although MW suggested they would be more difficult to arrange in T&W Division, because of the number of employees on the road.

It was agreed that

(a) in the same way that employee handbooks will differ in content, although following similar principles, each division will have to develop its own pattern of meetings, according to its circumstances;
(b) regular meetings may have to be supplemented for urgent business by occasional *ad hoc* meetings;
(c) tutorial groups for section managers on chairmanship will probably be required;
(d) divisions should proceed experimentally as soon as possible;
(e) the matter should be reviewed, with the aim of preparing guidelines, at the October meeting. [Action: All]

26/91 PAY NEGOTIATIONS (minute 13/91 refers)
The Chairman reported that all divisional pay negotiations have been completed and a confidential note on significant developments has been circulated to those concerned.

27/91 PAY SLIPS (minute 17/91 refers)
New style pay slips have been favourably received.

New items

28/91 RECRUITMENT AGE LIMITS
The Chief Executive wishes the Committee to examine the extent to which traditional recruitment practices in some divisions are

detrimental to well qualified job applicants over 50. The main points brought up in discussion were as follows.

(a) Some manual jobs are still restricted to younger male recruits, although, as a result of mechanisation, they no longer require much physical strength.
(b) Many managers and supervisors believe that younger recruits are more adaptable and are also reluctant to take charge of employees older than themselves.
(c) Executive applicants, previously in senior positions which have become redundant, present particular problems.
(d) In MW's view — not shared by others — older applicants who have spent most of their working lives in traditional industry have difficulty in meeting the challenge of a more demanding organisation.
(e) Practices within divisions vary and the picture is not sufficiently clear to form a judgement.

It was decided, therefore, to form a working group, comprising MW (Chairman) and one nominee each from FF and W&S Divisions, to investigate and report back at the next meeting. [Action: RD, JM and MW, to start by 8.4.91]

29/91 VIDEO LIBRARY

XYZ Training Videos have offered a demonstration showing, free of charge, of two new training videos, on Stress and on Alcoholism (both about 15 minutes duration). It was agreed that these could be useful additions to the Group Video Library and the company should be invited to show the videos at the July meeting. [Action: AW by 1.5.91]

30/91 COMPUTERISATION OF TRAINING RECORDS

Ms Anne Markleham from ABC Consultants gave a talk on recent developments in this field. Questions and discussion continued during lunch. (Copy of handout — Appendix 2)

Following Ms Markleham's departure, it was agreed that she had raised some interesting, but expensive, possibilities. The Chairman offered to make enquiries of two or three companies which have practical experience of various systems and report back at the July meeting. [Action: Chairman by 10.6.91]

31/91 CRAFT APPRENTICE AND GRADUATE TRAINEE INTAKE
The Chairman confirmed the instructions given by the Chief Executive to Divisional Managing Directors that, whatever cutbacks may be necessary in overall recruitment, there should be no reduction in the normal rate of craft apprentice and graduate trainee intake. It was generally agreed that this is a positive step, as it would help to avoid future shortages of skill and experience.

32/91 EMPLOYEE DISCOUNTS
JS said there are discrepancies between divisions in the rate of employee discounts on company products and suggested there should be a uniform rate. It was agreed to recommend to the Group Management Committee that a uniform rate of % (ie the rate – higher than the others – now enjoyed in FF and CP Divisions) should be applied throughout the Group. [Action: Chairman by 15.4.91]

33/91 FINANCIAL ADVICE TO EMPLOYEES [Late item]
HS gave details of an offer from LMN Finance to provide, at a nominal charge, impartial investment advice to employees who acquire substantial capital sums through, for example, Group sponsored savings schemes or redundancy payments, and invited other views before replying.

It was agreed, after discussion, that such offers should be declined, because,

(a) wholly impartial investment advice from a finance house, however reputable, is unlikely;
(b) any such arrangement would bear the stamp of Company approval and, because of the element of uncertainty in any investment, the Company might be indirectly blamed if the advice proved faulty.

It was, however, thought that there could be merit in an internal advisory service, which would explain to employees the pros and cons of various forms of investment, without indicating which might be preferable in individual cases.

The Chairman undertook to discuss the possibility with the Group Financial Director. [Action: Chairman by 1.5.91]

34/91 NEXT MEETING

The next meeting will be held at . . . . . on 5 July 1991, starting 10am (*not* 4 July, as originally arranged).

Index